Jolly Good Food

Enid Blyton

Jolly Good Food

ILLUSTRATED BY
MARK BEECH

RECIPES BY
ALLEGRA McEVEDY

Hodder
Children's
Books

Allegra McEvedy

Like many folks in our country, Enid Blyton was important to me when I was growing up: she was my first literary love. I gorged on the *Famous Five* and feasted on the *Secret Seven*, but my runaway fave was *The Naughtiest Girl in the School* – a fact that my father reminded me of by buying me a new copy on the day I got 'asked to leave' my posh secondary school some years later!

Blyton's storytelling is simple make-believe, but she had the knack of making her tales absolutely irresistible to young readers – and her descriptions of food were the same. The specifics she mentions are not elaborate – the opposite in fact – but the sheer pleasure she takes in everything from sardine sandwiches to cherry cake sings out of the pages.

After reading how the Famous Five sat on a rocky ledge eating tomato sandwiches, and about the ripe tomatoes grown in Mrs Lucy's shed in *Malory Towers*, I felt the urge to make a sandwich from the first decent tomatoes of the year that I'd been ripening on my kitchen table for a fortnight. Good, fresh white bread from the baker, a healthy amount of butter, ripe juicy tomatoes that look red but smell green, and a bit of salt and pepper. With the sun on your face, I don't think anything has ever tasted better.

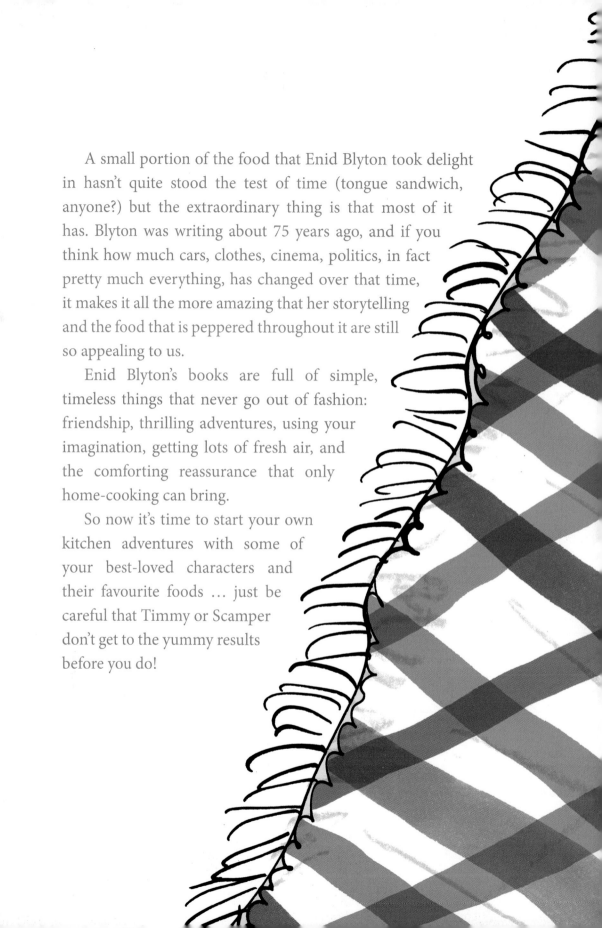

A small portion of the food that Enid Blyton took delight in hasn't quite stood the test of time (tongue sandwich, anyone?) but the extraordinary thing is that most of it has. Blyton was writing about 75 years ago, and if you think how much cars, clothes, cinema, politics, in fact pretty much everything, has changed over that time, it makes it all the more amazing that her storytelling and the food that is peppered throughout it are still so appealing to us.

Enid Blyton's books are full of simple, timeless things that never go out of fashion: friendship, thrilling adventures, using your imagination, getting lots of fresh air, and the comforting reassurance that only home-cooking can bring.

So now it's time to start your own kitchen adventures with some of your best-loved characters and their favourite foods … just be careful that Timmy or Scamper don't get to the yummy results before you do!

Contents

For the Twister – May 2017
A.McE.

Wherever eggs are used, they should be free-range – just as the Famous Five would have had on their picnics!

Breakfast
with the
Naughtiest
Girl

A Birthday Breakfast

Elizabeth went back to the bedroom. The breakfast-bell rang as she was tidying her chest-of-drawers. She slipped her arm through Joan's, and they went downstairs together. They stopped at the letter-rack. There was one card for Elizabeth from Mrs Allen – and in Joan's place were three envelopes, in which were the cards that Elizabeth had bought!

Joan took them down, going red with surprise. She opened them. She took out the first card and read it: 'With love, from Mother'. She turned to Elizabeth, her eyes shining.

'She's remembered my birthday!' she said to Elizabeth, and her voice was very happy. She was even more surprised when she found a card marked 'With love from Daddy', and she was delighted with Elizabeth's card.

'Fancy! Three cards!' said Joan, so happy that she didn't notice that the writing on the envelopes was the same for all three. She went into breakfast, quite delighted.

And on her chair was an enormous cardboard box from the baker, and a small neat parcel from the bookshop; Joan gave a cry of astonishment. 'More presents! Who from, I wonder?'

She opened the little parcel first, and when she saw the book about birds, and read the little card, her eyes filled suddenly with tears. She turned away to hide them. 'Look,' she whispered to Elizabeth, 'it's from my mother. Isn't it lovely of her to remember my birthday! I didn't think she would!'

Joan was so happy to have the book, which she thought came from her mother, that she almost forgot to undo the box in which was the enormous birthday cake.

'Undo this box, quickly,' begged Elizabeth.

Joan cut the string. She took off the lid, and everyone crowded round to see what was inside. When they saw the beautiful cake, they shouted in delight.

'Joan! What a fine cake! Oooh! You are lucky!'

Joan was too astonished to say a word. She lifted the cake out of the box, on its silver board, and stood it on the breakfast-table. She stared at it as if it was a dream cake. She couldn't believe it was really true.

'I say!' said Nora. 'What a cake! Look at the candles – and the sugar roses! And look at the message on it – "A happy birthday for my darling Joan!" Your mother has been jolly generous,

Joan – it's the biggest birthday cake I've seen.'

Joan stared at the message on the cake. She could hardly believe it. She felt so happy that she thought she would really have to burst. It was all so unexpected and so surprising.

Elizabeth was even happier – she looked at her friend's delighted face, and hugged herself for joy. She was glad she had spent all Uncle Rupert's ten-pound note on Joan. This was better than having a birthday herself – much, much better. Something that Miss Scott had often said to her flashed into her head.

'It is more blessed to give than to receive,' Miss Scott had said, when she had tried to make Elizabeth give some of her toys to the poor children at Christmas-time.

'And Miss Scott was quite right!' thought Elizabeth, in surprise. 'I'm getting more fun out of giving these things, than if I was receiving them myself!'

'Everybody in the school must share my birthday cake,' said Joan in a happy, important voice, and she lifted her head proudly, and smiled around.

'Thanks, Joan! Many happy returns of the day!' shouted everybody. And then Harry came in and cried, 'Joan! Shut your eyes and feel what I've got for you!'

In amazement Joan shut her eyes – and the next moment the

baby rabbit was in her arms. She gave a scream and opened her eyes again. She was so surprised that she didn't hold the rabbit tightly enough – and it leapt from her arms and scampered to the door, through which the teachers were just coming to breakfast.

The rabbit ran all round them, and the masters and mistresses stopped in astonishment.

'Is this a rabbit I see?' cried Mademoiselle, who was afraid of all small animals. 'Oh, these children! What will they bring to breakfast next?'

'I'm so sorry,' said Harry, catching the rabbit. 'You see, it's Joan's birthday, and I was giving her one of my rabbits.'

'I see,' said Miss Best. 'Well, take it out to the hutches now, Harry, and Joan can have it again after breakfast.'

'Oh, Elizabeth! I'm so happy!' whispered Joan, as they sat down to their eggs and bacon. 'I can't tell you how happy I am!'

'You needn't tell me,' said Elizabeth, laughing. 'I can see how happy you are – and I'm glad!'

from *The Naughtiest Girl in the School*
by Enid Blyton

PERFECT PORRIDGE *3 ways*

Ingredients

SERVES 4

100g rolled oats
200ml milk (I like proper blue top but it's also good with almond, if you want non-dairy)
200ml water
golden syrup, to serve (optional)

top of the milk/splash of cream, to serve (optional)

WITH BANANA, SULTANAS, CINNAMON AND MUSCOVADO:
2 bananas (the riper the better), sliced
30g sultanas
¼ tsp cinnamon
dark muscovado sugar, to your taste

Porridge Method

1 Put the oats, milk and water into a smallish pan with a thick bottom — too thin and your porridge will catch and burn easily.

2 Place the pan over a medium heat, stirring occasionally as it comes to the boil, then turn the heat down to the lowest setting and pop a lid on.

3 Cook for about 5 minutes like this, stirring occasionally so it doesn't stick on the bottom of the pan.

4 Check the consistency (which can vary wildly depending on the oats) — you want a nice, creamy texture so stir in a tablespoon more water if it's a bit thick. Enjoy with golden syrup or a splash of cream (or top of the milk), **or** try one of the following variations.

1 Start the porridge as in the method. When you turn the heat down, stir in the banana slices, sultanas and cinnamon, then put the lid on.

2 Cook for 5 minutes. Serve with a generous sprinkling of muscovado sugar on top.

For adventurous breakfasteers ...

WITH BACON AND MAPLE SYRUP:

1 tbsp vegetable or sunflower oil
180g unsmoked lardons or pancetta
 or streaky bacon, sliced
maple syrup

WITH BLUEBERRIES AND CREAM:

150g blueberries
couple of drops of vanilla extract
 (optional)
caster sugar, to your taste
double cream, to serve

1 First, get the porridge going as in the method. When the heat has been turned down and the lid's gone on, get on with making the topper.

2 In a frying pan, heat the oil and fry the bacon bits until crispy, stirring regularly.

3 Lift out with a slotted spoon on to kitchen paper to mop up the excess oil.

4 When the porridge is ready, scatter the bacon bits on top and drown in a pool of maple syrup!

1 Start the porridge as in the method. When you turn the heat down, chuck in two-thirds of the blueberries and the vanilla extract and give it a quick stir, then pop the lid on.

2 Cook for 5 minutes. Serve with the rest of the blueberries on top, a good sprinkling of caster sugar and a swirl of double cream to finish off the party.

DIPPY EGGS *with platoons of soldiers*

SERVES 4

Ingredients

4 medium eggs
dash of vinegar (any will do)

FOR THE HAM AND CHEESE SOLDIERS:
4 slices of white or brown bread
butter, softened, for spreading and frying
2 slices of ham
2 slices of Cheddar or Gruyère cheese

Eggs Method

1 Fill a medium-sized saucepan with water. The pan needs to be big enough for the eggs to be submerged. Add a dash of vinegar and bring the water to the boil.

2 As soon as it hits a busy rolling boil, carefully but quickly lower in the eggs one by one, using a slotted spoon, then reduce the heat to a simmer. Set your timer for 5 minutes for a firm egg white with a gooey yolk, or 6 minutes if you want a firmer yolk.

3 Sit the eggs in eggcups and carefully break open the top by smashing with the back of a teaspoon.

4 Pick off the bits of shell you've just cracked to reveal the crater-in-waiting ... Eat the top, then get dipping into the yellow lava.

1 To make the ham and cheese soldiers, spread the slices of bread with butter. Take two slices and top with the ham and cheese, then sandwich with another slice of bread on top.

2 Melt a lump of butter in a non-stick frying pan over a medium-high heat. When it's sizzling, put the sandwiches in the pan and fry for 3–4 minutes on each side, until they're evenly golden brown and crisp.

3 Lift them out of the pan and give them a good squish down with your hand (on the not-so-hot side) or with a plate, to compress, then use a breadknife to cut into soldiers.

FOR THE MAPLE BACON SOLDIERS
splash of vegetable oil, for frying
6 rashers of streaky bacon, smoked/
unsmoked
2 tbsp maple syrup

1 For the bacon, heat a medium-sized non-stick frying pan on a medium–high heat and add a tiny splash of oil. When it's hot, carefully lay in the bacon slices and fry for 3–4 minutes on each side until beautifully golden and starting to crisp.

2 When you're happy with the crispness and colour of your bacon, pour in the maple syrup. As it starts to bubble, use tongs to turn and roll the bacon around in the syrup for a couple of minutes until splendidly caramelised.

3 Turn the heat off, lift the bacon out and rest it on paper to mop up the excess oil/syrup.

FOR THE SEEDY MARMITE SOLDIERS
2 slices of white or brown bread
butter, softened, for spreading
1–2 tbsp Marmite, to your taste
1 tbsp mixed seeds such as sesame,
poppy, sunflower, pumpkin, anything you
fancy (optional but they're crunchy and healthy!)

1 For the Marmite dippers, simply toast the bread slices until golden, then spread with a little butter and Marmite. Sprinkle with your favourite mixed seeds and cut into soldiers.

FLUFFY PUFFY CHEESY PILLOWS

MAKES 8

(serves 4 people)

Ingredients

600g potatoes (suitable for mashing), peeled
3 eggs, separated
80g Cheddar cheese, grated
a few scrapings of fresh nutmeg or a pinch
 of ground nutmeg
20g unsalted butter
salt

OPTIONAL EXTRAS:

Crispy bacon
Fried eggs
Spinach
Ketchup!

Cheese

Method

1 First get your mash going. Cut the big spuds into quarters and the average-size ones in half, then put them in a large saucepan.

2 Pour on cold water to just cover them and chuck in a generous pinch of salt.

3 Stick a lid on and bring to a boil over a high heat. When bubbling away madly, take the lid off and turn down to a busy simmer for the 15–20 minutes it takes them to cook through. You can tell they're ready by sticking a small knife in one and lifting it just above the surface of the water with the knife pointing downwards. If the potato falls back in, it's ready; if it stays on, it's not; and if it breaks in two, it's overcooked (not a big problem, but it makes for less puffy pillows).

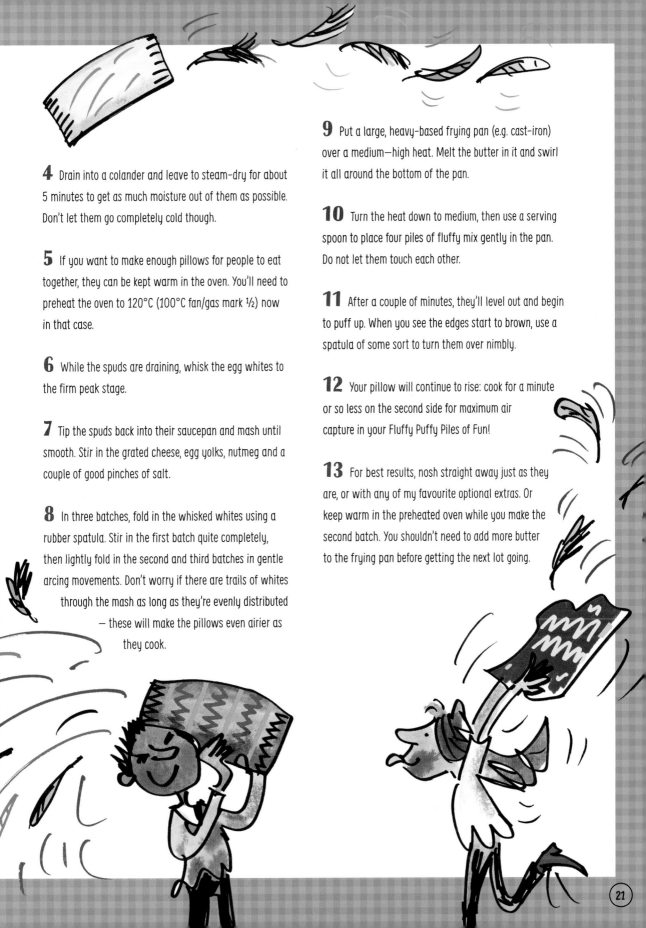

4 Drain into a colander and leave to steam-dry for about 5 minutes to get as much moisture out of them as possible. Don't let them go completely cold though.

5 If you want to make enough pillows for people to eat together, they can be kept warm in the oven. You'll need to preheat the oven to 120°C (100°C fan/gas mark ½) now in that case.

6 While the spuds are draining, whisk the egg whites to the firm peak stage.

7 Tip the spuds back into their saucepan and mash until smooth. Stir in the grated cheese, egg yolks, nutmeg and a couple of good pinches of salt.

8 In three batches, fold in the whisked whites using a rubber spatula. Stir in the first batch quite completely, then lightly fold in the second and third batches in gentle arcing movements. Don't worry if there are trails of whites through the mash as long as they're evenly distributed — these will make the pillows even airier as they cook.

9 Put a large, heavy-based frying pan (e.g. cast-iron) over a medium–high heat. Melt the butter in it and swirl it all around the bottom of the pan.

10 Turn the heat down to medium, then use a serving spoon to place four piles of fluffy mix gently in the pan. Do not let them touch each other.

11 After a couple of minutes, they'll level out and begin to puff up. When you see the edges start to brown, use a spatula of some sort to turn them over nimbly.

12 Your pillow will continue to rise: cook for a minute or so less on the second side for maximum air capture in your Fluffy Puffy Piles of Fun!

13 For best results, nosh straight away just as they are, or with any of my favourite optional extras. Or keep warm in the preheated oven while you make the second batch. You shouldn't need to add more butter to the frying pan before getting the next lot going.

BRILLIANT BREAKFAST BISCUITS *to make you bounce!*

MAKES 24

Ingredients

100g unsalted butter
60g demerara sugar
4 tbsp golden syrup
½ tsp vanilla extract
¼ tsp salt
100g oats

100g oatbran
50g sesame seeds
100g mixed nuts, chopped (whatever you fancy/ have in the cupboard, e.g. cashews, blanched almonds or hazelnuts etc.)
75g mixed dried fruit (more fun if you mix the usual sultanas and raisins with more unusual stuff like cranberries, dates, cherries etc.)
1 egg, beaten

Method

1 Preheat the oven to 180°C (160°C fan/gas mark 4) and line a large baking tray with baking paper.

2 In a small saucepan over a low–medium heat, melt together the butter, sugar, golden syrup, vanilla and salt.

3 Put all the remaining ingredients into a bowl and pour the melted contents of the pan over the top. Stir with a wooden spoon until well combined.

4 Using wet hands, pick up a walnut-sized amount of the mix and squish it between your palms so it sticks together into a ball.

5 Sit the ball on the baking tray, then gently press down with your palm to flatten it a bit. Repeat with the rest of the mix.

6 Put the tray on the middle shelf of the oven. After 6 minutes, turn the tray around to make sure the biscuits colour evenly. Bake for a further 4–6 minutes until the biscuits are brown and crispy at the edges.

7 When completely cooled, keep in an airtight container for up to 5 days — instant energy!

STACK O' DROP SCONES

MAKES 20

Ingredients

220g self-raising flour
30g unsalted butter, softened and roughly chopped + extra for frying and serving
2 tbsp caster sugar

2 eggs
1 tbsp golden syrup + plenty more for serving
½ tsp vanilla extract
200ml whole milk
salt

Method

1 In a mixing bowl, sift the flour, then add the butter. Using your fingertips, rub the butter into the flour until it looks like sandy breadcrumbs. Then stir in the sugar. Make a well in the middle and put it to one side.

2 In another little bowl, beat the egg. Add the golden syrup (it slips off the tablespoon into the bowl more easily if you put a little oil on the tablespoon first) and the vanilla and beat together. Pour this mixture into the hole you made in the flour/butter/sugar.

3 Tip the milk into the hole too, then use a wooden spoon to gradually start bringing the dry ingredients into the wet until the whole bowl is one smooth-ish batter.

4 Preheat the oven to 160°C (140°C fan/gas mark 3) if you want to keep the done ones warm and serve them all at the same time — not necessary if you're happy to dole them out as they're ready.

5 Heat a flat griddle pan or non-stick frying pan over a medium heat. Add a teaspoon of butter and swirl it around to melt evenly.

6 Using a tablespoon, drop four separate spoonfuls of the mix into the sizzling buttery pan.

7 Turn the heat right down and don't touch the scones until you see little bubbles appear on the surface and a slight browning at the edge, then flip over using a palette knife/fish slice/any kind of flippery thing.

8 Cook for slightly less time on the second side. Then either keep warm in the oven until you have enough for a proper stack, or sling them at your loved ones to nosh on straight away.

9 Enjoy with streams of melted butter and waterfalls of golden syrup.

SCRAMBLED EGGS
and garlic mushrooms on toast

Ingredients

250g mushrooms (chestnut mushrooms are nice but button are fine too — I'd pick the stalks out* but it's up to you)

3 large eggs

2 tbsp milk

2½ tbsp butter

1–2 garlic cloves, peeled and finely chopped (My six year-old daughter and I LOVE garlic but I do understand this is brekkie, so leave it out if you prefer)

salt and pepper

2 slices of bread, for toast

*Everyone's funny about something. My best friend can't be in the same room as a banana, my daughter loves rare steak but runs a mile at peas ... and my funny is mushroom stalks. There, now you know.

Method

1 Wash the mushrooms briefly under the tap, then cut into halves/quarters/thick slices depending on their size.

2 Get the egg mix ready: crack the eggs into a bowl and use a fork or whisk to beat together with the milk and a pinch of salt and some pepper if you fancy it.

3 Choose your best frying pan for the job — we're going to use the same one for the mushrooms and then the eggs, so it needs to be neither too big nor too small.

4 Melt 1½ tablespoons of the butter in the frying pan over a medium heat until sizzling, then chuck in the mushrooms. Don't play with them too much for the first couple of minutes — they need time to pick up a bit of colour from the bottom of the pan — then season with a pinch of salt and give them a stir.

5 When you can see they are nearly cooked — about 5 minutes — add the finely chopped garlic and stir it in well.

6 When you see the garlic flecks go from white to golden brown (won't take long at all), turn off the heat, spoon the mushrooms into a bowl and cover with foil.

7 There's no need to wash the frying pan — just ask a grown-up to wipe it out with some kitchen roll so there are no bits left in there.

8 Pop it back on a medium heat with the rest of the butter, and while it's melting, get the toast going.

9 Tip the pan around so it's evenly covered in butter, then pour in the beaten eggs. Use a rubber spatula to keep the setting eggs moving around so they don't brown. Turn the heat off after just a couple of minutes, as you want them to be creamy not rubbery.

10 Now for the big finish. Stick your toast on plates (no need to butter it — plenty of that in the rest of it), give the eggs a last proper scramble with the spatula to break up any big bits, put the eggs on the toast and add the mushrooms to finish.

HUZZAH!

OPTIONAL EXTRAS/VARIATIONS:

To make it more indulgent, add a splash of cream or spoonful of crème fraîche to the eggs at the end. And/or make your toast from brioche.
You could also stir in some cream cheese or grate on some Cheddar.

Or for a healthier tip, add a handful of spinach (cooked) or watercress (raw) — then you'll have protein, carbs and veg all on your plate.

RISE & SHINE SMOOTHIE

MAKES 4 SMALL GLASSES

Ingredients

1 mango
juice of 2 oranges
1 banana, peeled and sliced
300ml carrot juice or apple juice (bought!)

drizzle of honey (if using carrot juice)
2cm piece of ginger, peeled (optional)
handful of ice cubes

Method

1 Peel the mango and then cut all the flesh off it, going as close to the stone as you can. Pop the flesh in a tall jug blender or liquidizer. (Keep the stone for sucking and gnawing on later – delicious, if a little messy!)

2 Add the orange juice, banana, carrot or apple juice and a squidge of honey if using carrot juice. Finely grate in the ginger, if you like it fiery, and lastly chuck in a handful of ice cubes.

3 Whizz together until the mixture is silky smooth and electric orange!

4 Divide the smoothie between little glasses. Vibrant, fresh and packed full of goodness: the perfect way to rise and shine!

NAUGHTY & NICE SMOOTHIE

Ingredients

500ml semi-skimmed milk
200g natural yoghurt
2 bananas, peeled
4 tbsp smooth peanut butter
1 tbsp maple syrup or honey
few drops of vanilla extract

MAKES 4 SMALL GLASSES

Method

1 Pour the milk and yoghurt into a tall jug blender or liquidizer, along with the banana, peanut butter, maple syrup (or honey) and vanilla extract.

2 Blend together until it's frothy, creamy and smooth, then pour between little glasses. Tastes naughty but nice!

Elevenses
in the
Secret Seven's
Shed

The Secret Seven Meet

'Mummy, have you got anything we could have to drink?' asked Janet. 'And to eat too?'

'But you've only just finished your breakfast!' said their mother in surprise. 'And you each had two sausages. You can't possibly want anything more yet.'

'Well, we're having the very last meeting of the Secret Seven this morning,' said Janet. 'Down in the shed. We don't think it's worthwhile meeting when we all go back to school – nothing exciting ever happens then.'

'We're going to meet again when the Christmas holidays come,' said Peter. 'Aren't we, Scamper, old boy?'

The golden spaniel wagged his tail hard, and gave a small bark.

'He says, he hopes he can come to the last meeting too,' said Janet. 'Of course you can, Scamper.'

'He didn't say that,' said Peter, grinning. 'He said that if

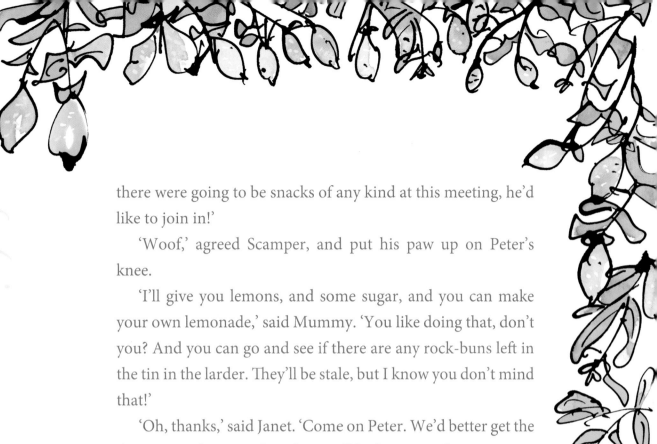

there were going to be snacks of any kind at this meeting, he'd like to join in!'

'Woof,' agreed Scamper, and put his paw up on Peter's knee.

'I'll give you lemons, and some sugar, and you can make your own lemonade,' said Mummy. 'You like doing that, don't you? And you can go and see if there are any rock-buns left in the tin in the larder. They'll be stale, but I know you don't mind that!'

'Oh, thanks,' said Janet. 'Come on Peter. We'd better get the things now, because the others will be here soon!'

They ran off to the larder, Scamper panting behind. Rock-buns! Stale or not, Scamper liked those as much as the children did.

Janet took some lemons, and went to get the sugar from her mother. Peter emptied the stale rock-buns on to a plate, and the two of them, followed by Scamper, went down to the shed. Janet had the lemon-squeezer and a big jug of water. It was fun to make lemonade.

They pushed open the shed door. On it were the letters S.S. in green – S.S. for the Secret Seven!

'Our Secret Society has been going for some time now,' said

Janet, beginning to squeeze a lemon. 'I'm not a bit tired of it, are you, Peter?'

'Of course not!' said Peter. 'Just think of all the adventures we've had, and the exciting things we've done! But I do think it's sensible not to bother about the Secret Seven meetings till the hols. For one thing, in this Christmas term the days get dark very quickly, and we have to be indoors.'

'Yes, and nothing much happens then,' said Janet. 'Oh, Scamper – you won't like that squeezed-out lemon-skin, you silly dog! Drop it!'

Scamper dropped it. He certainly didn't like it! He sat with his tongue hanging out, looking most disgusted.

from *Secret Seven on the Trail*
by *Enid Blyton*

TRIPLY CHEESY STRAWS

Ingredients

plain flour, for dusting
320–375g ready-rolled puff pastry
100g of your favourite firm cream cheese
  (such as Boursin)

50g Cheddar cheese, grated
50g Red Leicester cheese, grated
pinch of sweet smoked paprika, if you fancy a
  little hit of spice
1 egg yolk, beaten with 1 tbsp milk ('eggwash')
pepper

Method

1 Preheat the oven to 200°C (180°C fan/gas mark 6) and line a large baking tray with baking paper.

2 Scatter a handful of flour on your work surface, then carefully unroll the puff pastry sheet and peel off the paper. Lay the rectangular piece of pastry vertically so one of the shorter sides is closest to you.

3 Use a rolling pin to roll the pastry out a little more so it's a touch thinner, still keeping the rectangular shape.

4 Using a palette knife, spread the cream cheese over the pastry, making sure you keep a 1–2cm border clear around the edge.

5 Scatter both kinds of grated cheese over the top, then sprinkle on the smoked paprika if using and season with pepper.

6 Cut the pastry lengthways (vertically) into 10 long strips, so each strip is about 3cm wide. Then halve each one widthways to make 20 shorter strips.

7 Holding each strip by one end, twist the other end around as few or as many times as you like. Then, place it on the prepared baking tray and press each end down a bit on the tray to stop it unravelling.

8 Brush the pastry twists generously with the eggwash to glaze, then bake in the oven for 15–20 minutes until beautifully golden and crisp.

9 Eat warm or at room temperature. To make a big impression for serving, build a tower by stacking up your triply cheesy straws – magnificent!

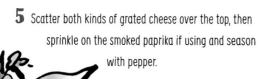

RAINBOW VEGGIE SKEWERS *with cream cheese and pesto dip*

SERVES 8

Ingredients

FOR THE VEGGIE SKEWERS:

50ml olive oil

2 tsp honey

dash of balsamic or red wine vinegar

1 lemon

2 small red onions, peeled and cut into little wedges

2 medium courgettes, cut into chunky half-moons

1 red pepper, deseeded and cut into chunks

1 yellow pepper, deseeded and cut into chunks

200g cherry tomatoes

salt and pepper

Very good with chicken or fish too!

FOR THE DIP:

200g cream cheese

100g natural yoghurt

squeeze of lemon juice

3 tbsp green (or red) pesto, whichever you fancy

You will need 8 wooden skewers. Soak them in cold water for 30 minutes before you start, to prevent them from burning.

Method

1 To make the veggie skewers, first mix the olive oil, honey and vinegar in a large bowl. Add the zest (finely-grated peel) from the lemon and a good squeeze of lemon juice, then season with a bit of salt and pepper. Mix together.

2 Drop the cut veg into the bowl and stir well to coat in the dressing. Leave the veggies to marinate while you knock up the dip.

3 Whisk the cream cheese in a medium bowl to soften, then switch to a wooden spoon to beat in the yoghurt. Finally stir in a squeeze of lemon juice, the pesto and a bit of salt and pepper to taste.

4 Evenly divide the vegetables between the wooden skewers, threading them on in any order you wish, until you've used up all your veg.

5 Heat a griddle pan or large non-stick frying pan over a high heat. If your pan is not big enough to hold all the skewers at the same time, put the oven on now at 120°C (100°C fan/gas mark ½), so you can keep the first batch warm when you're cooking the rest.

6 When your pan is good and hot, use tongs to carefully place the rainbow skewers in the pan. They can be close but not touching.

7 Cook over a medium—high heat for about 5 minutes on each side, turning frequently and carefully until all the veggies are softened, lightly charred and gorgeously caramelised all over.

8 You can either dunk the skewers in the dip or splodge the dip all over the skewers — either way it's all rainbow goodness!

HONEY-ONION SAUSAGE ROLLS

Ingredients

20g butter + extra for greasing
splash of vegetable oil, for frying
2 medium red onions (about 280g), peeled
  and finely chopped
2 garlic cloves, peeled and finely chopped

1½ tbsp runny honey
flour, for dusting
320—375g ready-rolled puff pastry
350g sausage meat
1 egg yolk, beaten with 1 tbsp milk ('eggwash')
salt and pepper

Method

1 In a wide saucepan or frying pan, melt the butter in a little splash of oil over a medium heat. As it starts to sizzle, tip in the chopped onions and garlic.

2 Give them a bit of a stir every now and then, until they start to soften — about 7 minutes.

3 Stir in the honey, add a pinch of salt and turn the heat up a bit.

4 Keep stirring as the onions start to go slightly brown around the edges, then turn the heat off and set them aside to cool completely.

5 Preheat the oven to 180°C (160°C fan/gas mark 4) and lightly grease a large baking tray with a knob of butter.

6 Scatter a handful of flour on your work surface, then carefully unroll the pre-rolled pastry sheet and peel off the paper. Lay the rectangular piece of pastry horizontally so that one of the long sides is closest to you.

7 Using a small knife, halve it lengthways across the middle so you have two separate rectangles.

8 Move them apart, then roll a rolling pin up and down each half a few times, until each one is 5 or 6cm taller but no longer.

9 Mix the cooled onions with the sausage meat and a touch of salt, and divide the mixture into two equal piles.

10 Spread one of your meat piles in an even line just below the middle of one of the pastry rectangles.

11 Brush the flap of pastry nearest you with eggwash, then bring the far side of pastry over the meat to join the near side and tuck it in tightly under the sausage log. Roll the whole thing towards you so the join is on the underside. Give it a gentle squeeze down to compress and seal the edge underneath.

12 With a sharp knife trim the ends off the log, then lightly score the top of the pastry with diagonal lines all along the length of the log (do not cut deeply enough to go right through to the meat).

13 Put your four fingers together, lay them on top of the log, and cut it into rolls four fingers long.

14 Repeat with the other piece of pastry and the rest of meat.

15 Finally, move all the sausage rolls on to the greased tray and give them a good brush with eggwash before popping them in the oven for about 25 minutes.

16 When they are a lovely golden-brown, take them out of the oven and leave to cool a bit — yummy when warm, or top snacking from the fridge when cold.

JAM TARTS

MAKES 24

Ingredients

FOR THE PASTRY:

225g plain flour + extra for dusting
110g cold unsalted butter, cut into little
  cubes
25g caster sugar
1 orange
1 egg, beaten
sea salt

Or if you're in a hurry just buy a 300—320g packet of
ready-made sweet pastry and start from Step 5.

FOR THE FILLING:

24 generous teaspoons of your favourite
  jams (strawberry, raspberry, blackberry,
  apricot — a mix of colours is good)

1 egg yolk, beaten with 1 tbsp milk ('eggwash')

You will need two 12-hole tart tins and a
fluted or plain round cutter about 6—7cm
across (or roughly 1cm bigger than the tart
tin holes).

Method

1 To make the pastry, place the flour in a large bowl
and add the cold butter cubes. Using your fingertips, rub
the butter into the flour until the mixture resembles fine
breadcrumbs.

2 Stir in the caster sugar, a pinch of salt and little
sprinkle of zest (finely grated peel) from the orange.

3 Pour in the beaten egg and, using your hands or a
normal knife, quickly and evenly distribute the egg
through the mix.

4 Bring the pastry together into a ball and wrap
it in cling film. Pop it in the fridge and chill for
about 30 minutes or a little longer if you have time.

5 Preheat the oven to 180°C (160°C fan/ gas mark 4). When you're ready to make the tarts, take the pastry from the fridge and remove the cling film. Scatter a handful of flour on your work surface and roll the pastry out until about 0.5cm thick.

6 Using your pastry cutter, stamp out 24 rounds of pastry. Gently press one into each hole in the tins, pushing it carefully into the base and up the sides. Re-roll any pastry as you need. (You'll have a little nugget of pastry left over but keep it in the freezer for another time or just keep making more tarts!)

7 Prick the base of each tart case with a fork, then spoon a generous teaspoon of jam into each one, remembering to swap flavours as you go.

8 Using a pastry brush, brush the top of the pastry edge with the eggwash, which makes it nice and golden and shiny when it's baked.

9 Pop in the oven and bake for 12–15 minutes until the pastry is beautifully crisp and golden and the gooey jam all bubbling and oozy.

10 Take them out of the oven and leave to sit in the tin for a couple of minutes, then use a palette knife to get them on to a wire rack to cool a bit. Jam straight from the oven is hotter than you expect!

ROCK BUNS

MAKES 12

Ingredients

225g plain flour
125g unsalted butter, cold and cut into
    smallish cubes
100g caster sugar
1 tsp baking powder

100g dried mixed fruit (any of your favourite ones)
50g currants
½ tsp mixed spice
1 medium egg, beaten
splash of milk (about 1 tbsp)
demerara sugar, for sprinkling

Method

1 Preheat the oven to 180°C (160°C fan/gas mark 4) and line a large baking tray (or a couple of smaller ones) with baking paper.

2 Tip the flour into a large bowl along with the cubed butter. Using your fingertips, rub the butter into the flour until it resembles fine breadcrumbs.

3 Add the caster sugar, baking powder, dried fruit, currants and mixed spice and stir with a wooden spoon until well combined. Pour in the beaten egg and a splash of milk and stir to make a stiff dough.

4 Spoon 12 rocky heaps on to the prepared trays, making sure you space them out evenly to allow room for a bit of spreading during baking. Keep them all lumpy and bumpy looking for a rough finish.

5 Scatter a generous sprinkle of demerara sugar over the heaps and bake in the oven for 15–20 minutes until they are lightly golden.

6 Take them out of the oven, and after about 5 minutes move them on to a wire rack to cool a bit. Good just like that or broken open and eaten warm with slatherings of butter — much tastier than when stale, despite what the Secret Seven think!

THE SECRET SEVEN'S GINGERBREAD SHED

Ingredients

FOR THE GINGERBREAD:

100g light muscovado sugar
½ tsp mixed spice
½ tsp ground ginger
4 tbsp golden syrup
125g unsalted butter
300g plain flour

1 tsp bicarbonate of soda
1 small orange

FOR THE ICING:

1 egg white
200g icing sugar, sifted

You will need a piping bag.

SUGGESTED DECORATIONS: chocolate buttons, chocolate fingers, jelly diamonds, gold balls etc.

Method

1 Preheat the oven to 200°C (180°C fan/gas mark 6) and line two large baking sheets with baking paper.

2 Put the sugar, spices, syrup and butter in a medium–large pan and bring to a gentle simmer. Give it a stir and, when the butter has melted, turn off the heat and allow to cool slightly.

3 In a large bowl, mix together the flour and bicarbonate of soda and add the zest (finely grated peel) from a small orange.

4 Pour in the melted butter mixture and then stir with a wooden spoon to bring it together into a rough dough. Divide the dough into six even pieces (around 100g each).

5 Trace the templates on the next page and carefully cut out the sections to give you 2 x roof panels, 2 x side panels and 2 x front/back panels.

6 Arrange a sheet of baking paper (about 25cm square) on a flat surface. Put one of the dough pieces on top, then cover with another sheet of baking paper and, using a rolling pin, roll out the dough between the paper until it is roughly in a rectangle just bigger than one of the templates.

7 Repeat this step with all the dough, until you have rolled out six flat pieces.

8 Use the templates to cut each of your 6 dough pieces to the right size and shape. Then transfer your shed pieces to lined baking sheets.

9 You'll have a bunch of dough offcuts, which you can squidge into a ball. Either freeze for another time or use it to make some gingerbread Secret Seven characters to hang out in the shed. Roll the dough out again to about 0.5cm thick, then use a small gingerbread person cutter (not the standard size) to cut these out. Leave in the fridge until you've cooked all the shed gingerbread.

10 Cook the shed pieces in the oven for 10–12 minutes until light golden brown and starting to go dark around the edges.

11 Meanwhile, put any gingerbread people you've made on trays lined with baking paper and bake for 8–10 minutes until light golden brown, and beginning to darken around the edges.

12 To make the icing that will be the glue/cement, whisk the egg white with an upright mixer or electric whisk until starting to foam, then add the icing sugar and whip again until very stiff and glossy. Use a rubber spatula (and another pair of hands!) to get it into a piping bag.

13 When the gingerbread is completely cold, start making your shed. First, you want to build your walls, so work out which are your roof pieces and set them aside. Pipe icing along the wall edges and connect the walls by gently pressing them together. Leave this to set for a couple of hours.

14 When the walls are firm, carefully pipe along the edges of the roof panels and press gently to sit on top. Leave for another couple of hours to set completely.

15 Now it's time for the fun! Decorate the shed with whatever you fancy. You can use icing to stick chocolate fingers and chocolate buttons to the roof, or jelly diamonds to the sides to make pretty windows. You can stick on decorations with icing, or just use it to draw windows, doors, tiling and whatever else you feel like. Happy building!

SHED CONSTRUCTION TEMPLATES

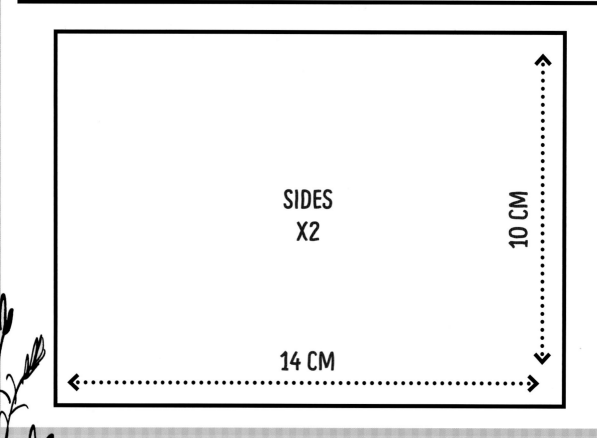

ROOF
X2

10 CM

16 CM

SIDES
X2

10 CM

14 CM

You will need to make three different templates
to assemble your shed. Using baking paper, a ruler, pencil
and pair of scissors, trace and cut out the following 6
pieces (2 of each), making sure you label each one:
ROOF, SIDES AND FRONT/BACK.

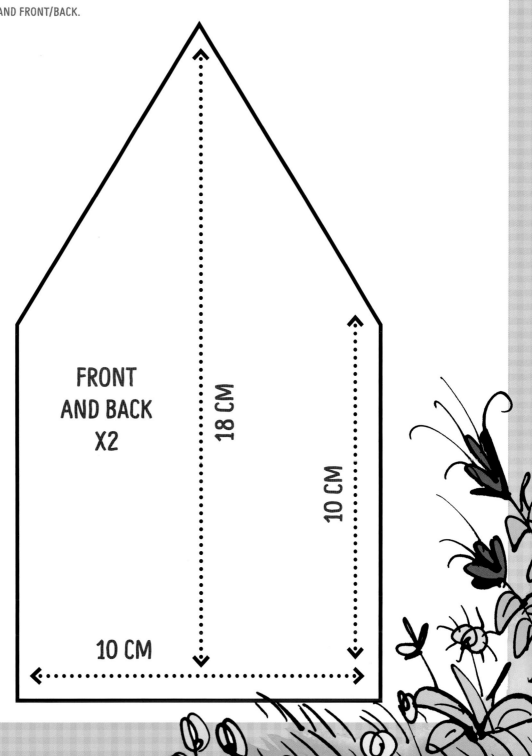

FRONT
AND BACK
X2

18 CM

10 CM

10 CM

LIP-SMACKING LEMONADE

MAKES
5 TALL
GLASSES

Ingredients

3 lemons
2 limes
100g caster sugar
few handfuls of ice

TOP TIP: When you've drunk all the lemonade, don't throw away the citrus, but refill the jug with water, adding some mint, strawberries, cucumber or orange slices, and pop it in the fridge to make some nice cold fruity water for later/tomorrow.

Method

1 First, juice the lemons and limes — you should end up with about 150–200ml of juice in total, depending on the juiciness of the fruit, so add the juice of another lemon if you don't have enough. Keep the squeezed-out lemon and lime skins for infusion in the jug later.

2 Put this juice in a jar with the sugar and 250ml of water, screw the lid on tightly and ... shake, shake, shake it until the sugar has dissolved completely: a good 2 or 3 minutes of business.

3 Pour it into a large jug with 1 litre of cold water. Add the squeezed-out lemon and lime skins (which will give it a zesty flavour) and some ice.

ZING-A-LICIOUS!

Picnicking
with
The Famous
Five

Five Have a Lovely Picnic

They stopped at a tiny village called Manlington-Tovey. It had only one general store, but it sold practically everything – or seemed to! 'Hope it sells ginger beer!' said Julian. 'My tongue's hanging out like Timmy's!'

The little shop sold lemonade, orangeade, lime juice, grapefruit juice and ginger beer. It was really difficult to choose which to have. It also sold ice-creams, and soon the children were sitting drinking ginger beer and lime juice mixed, and eating delicious ices.

'Timmy must have an ice,' said George. 'He does so love them. Don't you, Timmy?'

'Woof,' said Timmy, and gulped his ice down in two big, gurgly licks.

'It's really a waste of ice-creams to give them to Timmy,' said Anne. 'He hardly has time to taste them, he gobbles them

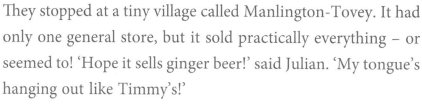
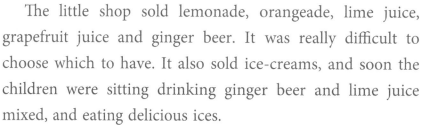

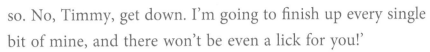

so. No, Timmy, get down. I'm going to finish up every single bit of mine, and there won't be even a lick for you!'

Timmy went off to drink from a bowl of water that the shopwoman had put down for him. He drank and he drank, then he flopped down, panting.

The children took a bottle of ginger beer each with them when they went off again. They meant to have it with their lunch. Already they were beginning to think with pleasure of eating the sandwiches put up into neat packets for them.

Anne saw some cows pulling at the grass in a meadow as they passed. 'It must be awful to be a cow and eat nothing but tasteless grass,' she called to George. 'Think what a cow misses – never tastes an egg and lettuce sandwich, never eats a chocolate éclair, never has a boiled egg – and can't even drink a glass of ginger beer! Poor cows!'

George laughed. 'You do think of silly things, Anne,' she said. 'Now you've made me want my lunch all the more – talking about egg sandwiches and ginger beer! I know Mother made us egg sandwiches – and sardine ones too.'

'It's no good,' chimed in Dick, leading the way into a little copse, his bicycle wobbling dangerously. It's no good – we can't go another inch if you girls are going to jabber about food all the time. Julian, what about lunch?'

It was a lovely picnic, that first one in the copse. There were clumps of primroses all round, and from somewhere nearby came the sweet scent of hidden violets. A thrush was singing madly on a hazel tree, with two chaffinches calling 'pink-pink' every time he stopped.

'Band and decorations laid on,' said Julian, waving his hand towards the singing birds and the primroses. 'Very nice too. We just want a waiter to come and present us with a menu!'

A rabbit lolloped near, its big ears standing straight up inquiringly. 'Ah – the waiter!' said Julian, at once. 'What have you to offer us today, Bunny? A nice rabbit-pie?'

The rabbit scampered off at top speed. It had caught the smell of Timmy nearby and was panic-stricken. The children laughed, because it seemed as if it was the mention of rabbit-pie that had sent it away. Timmy stared at the disappearing rabbit, but made no move to go after it.

'Well, *Timmy!* That's the first time you've ever let a rabbit go off on its own,' said Dick. 'You *must* be hot and tired. Got anything for him to eat, George?'

'Of course,' said George. 'I made his sandwiches myself.'

And so she had! She had bought sausage meat at the butcher's and had actually made Timmy twelve sandwiches

with it, all neatly cut and packed.

The others laughed. George never minded taking trouble over Timmy. He wolfed his sandwiches eagerly, and thumped his tail hard on the mossy ground. They all sat and munched happily, perfectly contented to be together out in the open air, eating a wonderful lunch.

Anne gave a scream. 'George! Look what you're doing! You're eating one of Timmy's sandwiches!'

'Urhh!' said George. 'I thought it tasted a bit strong. I must have given Timmy one of mine and taken his instead. Sorry, Tim!'

'Woof,' said Tim politely, and accepted another of his sandwiches.

from *Five Get Into Trouble*
by Enid Blyton

BLOOMER LOAF

bloomin' gorgeous loaf

Ingredients

500g strong white bread flour + extra for
 dusting
1½ tsp salt

7g sachet fast-action dried yeast
4 tbsp olive oil + extra for greasing
300ml lukewarm water

Method

1 Place the flour in a large bowl (or free-standing electric mixer with dough hook attachment if you have one) and add the salt and yeast. Drizzle in the olive oil and add the lukewarm water (too hot and it will kill the yeast, too cold and it won't activate it).

2 Bring the mixture together in the good old-fashioned way using your hands (or whizz speedily in the machine) and keep working it until you have a soft dough, adding a splash of extra water if you think it needs it to stick together. Shape the dough roughly into a ball.

3 If kneading by hand, scatter a handful of flour on your work surface and knead the dough for about 10 minutes or so (quite a workout!), until you have a soft, smooth and elastic dough that gently bounces back to the touch. If using the mixer, knead the dough on medium speed for a good 5 minutes.

4 Put your super-smooth dough ball into a lightly floured or oiled large clean bowl and leave to prove (rise) for about an hour in a warm place. It should double in size and be springy and light to the touch like a sponge cake.

5 Lightly flour your work surface again. Tip the dough out of the bowl and 'knock it back' by giving it a good 'knock' with the heel of your hands, kneading it and pushing out any air bubbles.

6 Now shape your loaf. First, flatten it into a rough oval. Keep the long side facing you and fold each end into the middle, then turn it over to the other side so you have a smooth top and the folded seam running along the bottom. Gently rock and roll it back and forth to create a smooth, oval-shaped bloomer.

7 Sit the bread on a large baking tray or flat sheet lined with baking paper and cover with a clean tea towel. Leave to prove again in the same warm place for about 1½ hours until it's doubled in size.

8 Preheat the oven to 220°C (200°C fan/gas mark 7).

9 When the dough is ready, lightly dust the top of the loaf with a touch of flour and lightly cut a few diagonal or straight slashes across the top using a sharp knife.

10 Bake the bloomer in the hot oven for 20 minutes, then lower the heat to 200°C (180°C fan/gas mark 6) and bake for a further 10–20 minutes until golden brown with a crispy crust.

11 Take it out of the oven and tuck in – freshly baked warm bread with loads of melting butter is bloomin' delicious! Once cold, try toasting it with the smoked mackerel pâté over the page.

SMOKED MACKEREL PÂTÉ

SERVES 5

Famously!

Ingredients

150g smoked mackerel fillets, skin pulled off
100g cream cheese
juice of ½ lemon (to taste)
pepper

TO SERVE:
bloomer, granary or seeded bread
cucumber slices or pieces of red pepper

This is one of the shortest recipes in the book ... and possibly the yummiest!

Makes a small bowlful — enough for a round of sarnies each for the Famous Five, and Timmy can lick the bowl.

Method

1 Briefly run the tips of your fingers over the surface of the fish to check if any bones are sticking out — there shouldn't be, but crunching on bits of bones is a sure way to ruin a great pâté.

2 Put the smoked mackerel into the food processor and spin for a minute until the fish has gone fluffy (sounds strange but you'll know what I mean when you see it).

3 Tip in the cream cheese and some of the lemon juice (but not all of it to start with) and whizz for a few more seconds.

4 Turn the food processor off and have a taste. Season to your liking with more lemon juice and some ground black pepper if you like it (grown-ups definitely will if you're making it for them too).

5 Make your picnic sandwiches on fresh bloomer bread with cucumber … or ditch the bread and try it as a summery snack piled on slices of cucumber or red pepper. But in winter it has to be served on hot buttered toast — YUM!

FIVE FAMOUS QUICHES

EACH
SERVES
8

Ingredients

FOR PASTRY BASE (SAME FOR ALL FIVE RECIPES):
300—320g ready-rolled shortcrust pastry
1 egg

You'll need a fluted tart case with a push-up base (24cm across x 3cm deep).

Or, if you want to make your own pastry, use the recipe from the clementine treacle tart on page 90, but replace the icing sugar with 60g of plain flour, and add 2 tbsp of cold water, a pinch of salt and a grind of pepper.

Pastry Method

1 Preheat the oven to 190°C (170°C fan/gas mark 5)

2 Lightly flour your work surface and roll out the pastry to about half a centimetre thick.

3 Lay it into the tart case, pushing it well into the corner around the base. Then using the top third of your fingers, press the pastry into the upright fluted edge all the way round so that it's firmly held and not too thick.

4 Sit your rolling pin on top of the tart case and gently roll it along the top so that the excess pastry falls off.

5 Prick the base all over with a fork then line with greaseproof paper, fill it with baking beans and put it on the bottom shelf of the oven for 10-12 mins.

6 Carefully lift out the greaseproof paper and baking beans, setting aside the beans to cool before putting away to reuse. Then turn the pastry case around so it colours evenly.

7 Cook for just another 5 minutes, and during this time separate the egg. Whip the white with a fork until loose and frothy, and keep the yolk for the tart middle later.

8 Lift the pastry case out, give it a thorough brush all over with the beaten white and then put it back again for 5 mins for this glaze to set hard and shiny.

9 Take the case out and turn the oven down to 180°C (160°C fan/gas mark 4) - the right temp to cook the quiche on.

10 Your tart case is now ready for its filling!

Choose one of the following delicious fillings for your case:

SALMON, BROCCOLI & CREAM CHEESE QUICHE

Ingredients

100g tenderstem broccoli, cut into 2cm pieces

220g (approx.) salmon, skinned and boned, cut into 2–3cm pieces

3 eggs + the yolk left over from glazing the tart case

200ml double cream

100g cream cheese

salt (and pepper – optional)

Method

1 Bring a pan of water to the boil with a pinch of salt, then drop the broccoli in it. As soon as it comes back to the boil (just a minute or two), drain the broccoli into a sieve and run cold water over it until it is completely cooled.

2 Pat the broccoli dry with kitchen roll, then scatter the raw salmon and broccoli bits all mixed up on the bottom of the cooked tart case.

3 In a jug or bowl, beat together the whole eggs, extra yolk, cream, cream cheese and a couple of good pinches of salt (and pepper too if you fancy it).

4 Pour this over the salmon and broccoli, so the case is filled right up to the top but not spilling over.

5 Sit it evenly on a baking tray and bake in the middle of the oven for 25–30 minutes, turning halfway through, until the outside is set but the inside still has a little wobble.

CHEDDAR, ONION & POTATO QUICHE

Ingredients

400g potatoes, peeled and thinly sliced
1 heaped tbsp butter
1 large or 2 medium onions (about 300g),
    peeled and sliced

120g Cheddar cheese, grated
150ml double cream
3 eggs + the yolk left over from glazing
    the tart case
salt and pepper

Method

1 Put the sliced potatoes into a saucepan and cover with cold water. Add a good pinch of salt.

2 Put a lid on, bring to the boil, then turn the heat down to a simmer. Leave to gently bubble for about 12 minutes until the spuds are soft when you stick a normal knife in them.

3 While the potatoes are cooking, melt the butter in a wide frying pan over a high heat. As it starts to sizzle, swirl it round the pan, then drop in the sliced onions and season with a couple of pinches of salt.

4 Stir regularly, keeping the heat high for a good 5 minutes until the onions have started to soften and colour a bit, then turn the heat down to medium for about another 10 minutes, stirring regularly until they are golden brown, soft and sweet.

5 Keep an eye on the spuds and when they're cooked, drain into a colander and leave to steam-dry for about 5 minutes.

6 When both the onions and spuds are ready, put half the spuds on the bottom of the tart case, then half the onions, topped by half the cheese.

7 Whisk together the cream, the whole eggs and the extra yolk from earlier, along with some salt and pepper.

8 Pour half of this mix into the tart case, then repeat with another potato, onion and cheese layering.

9 Finish with the rest of the creamy egg mix, so the case is filled to the top but not spilling over. Give the tin a quick shuffle to make sure that the cream fills all the holes.

10 Sit it evenly on a baking tray and bake in the middle of the oven for 25–30 minutes, turning halfway through, until evenly golden brown and puffed up.

11 Leave to cool for about 5 minutes before tucking in. Also ideal cold for a picnic, of course!

CHICKEN, PEA & PARMESAN QUICHE

Ingredients

150g cooked chicken (such as leftovers from a roast), roughly cut into small pieces

100g frozen peas, defrosted

3 eggs + the yolk left over from glazing the tart case

200ml double cream

30g Parmesan cheese, finely grated

salt and pepper

Method

1 Put the chicken and peas all mixed up on the bottom of the tart case.

2 Beat the eggs and mix them with the cream. Season with salt and pepper. Pour this mixture over the chicken and peas, so the case is filled right up to the top but not spilling over.

3 Finish by scattering the Parmesan on top, then pop on to a level baking tray and bake in the middle of the oven for 25–30 minutes, turning halfway through, until cooked to an even golden brown.

SAUSAGE & LEEK QUICHE

Ingredients

400g leeks

30g butter

2 garlic cloves, peeled and finely chopped
  (optional but delicious)

200g sausage meat

150ml double cream

3 eggs + the yolk left over from glazing the
  tart case

25g Parmesan cheese, finely grated

1 tbsp sweet mustard (e.g. German hotdog
  mustard)

6 cherry tomatoes, halved

salt

Method

1 Cut the leeks in half lengthways, all the way from the root end (but not through it) to green end.

2 Thinly slice them widthways, put into a colander and wash very well under cold running water. Leave to drain.

3 Melt the butter in a wide frying or saucepan over a medium–high heat. When it's sizzling, tip in the leeks.

4 Season with a bit of salt and keep stirring from time to time for the 10–12 minutes it takes the leeks to soften and cook.

5 While the leeks are cooking, roll the sausage meat into 10 balls of about 20g each.

6 Whisk together the eggs, cream, Parmesan, mustard and a couple of decent pinches of salt.

7 Put the cooked leeks in the bottom of the tart case, then dot the sausage balls in a circle around the outside.

8 Pour in the creamy egg mix nearly to the top of the tart case, then arrange the cherry tomatoes in two rings, one inside the other.

9 Sit it evenly on a baking tray and bake in the middle of the oven for 25–30 minutes, turning halfway through, until golden brown all over.

BAKED BEAN & BACON QUICHE

Ingredients

1 tbsp vegetable or sunflower oil
180g unsmoked lardons
1 tin (415g) baked beans

3 eggs + the yolk left over from glazing the tart case
150ml double cream
100g Cheddar cheese, grated
salt

Method

1 Pour the oil into a frying pan set over a high heat. When it's hot, fry the lardons for 5–6 minutes until browning.

2 Lift out with a slotted spoon, then drain on kitchen paper to remove any excess oil.

3 Drain (or eat) about 2 tbsp of the tomatoey juice at the top of the tin of baked beans, then tip the contents of the tin into the bottom of the prepared tart case.

4 Beat the eggs with the cream, cheese and a pinch of salt.

5 Scatter the crispy bacon bits on to the beans, then pour on the creamy egg mix, so the case is filled right up to the top but not spilling over.

6 Transfer to a level baking tray and bake in the middle of the oven for 30–35 minutes, turning halfway through, until golden brown all over.

Nursery food for sure ... super-easy eating!

OVEN-BAKED SCOTCH EGGS

Ingredients

5 eggs
dash of vinegar (any will do)
400g sausage meat

2 tbsp flour
80g dried breadcrumbs (panko breadcrumbs, found in the Asian section in supermarkets, are particularly good)
40g butter, melted
salt and pepper

Method

1 Put four of the eggs in a saucepan, cover with cold water, add a dash of vinegar and bring to the boil. As soon as it hits a busy rolling boil, turn the heat off and leave the eggs in the water for 6 minutes (set your timer).

2 When the timer goes off, tip the eggs into the sink — water and all — making sure that their shells crack as they land (to make them easier to peel later). Pop the eggs back into their pan and run cold water over them until they are completely cold when you hold one in your hand.

3 Gently peel the eggs — try to break the membrane under the shell for an easier job.

4 Lay four squares of cling film out flat in front of you and divide the sausage meat into four equal balls, placing each one on a piece of cling film.

5 Wet the palm of your hand and flatten each ball into a disc about 15cm across but a little thicker in the middle and thinner around the edges. Sit a peeled egg in the middle of each one.

6 Use the cling film to pick up the meat and shape it around the egg until it is completely covered. Take a moment to distribute the meat evenly around the egg, sealing all joining edges smoothly, and then get on with the next one.

7 Rest the cling film wrapped balls in the freezer for 20 minutes to firm up and preheat the oven to 220°C (200°C fan/gas mark 7).

8 Meanwhile, get your breadcrumbing station ready. Start with three wide, shallow bowls, plates or small trays. Tip the flour into the first one. Crack the last egg into the second and whisk lightly with a tablespoon of water. The breadcrumbs go into the third one.

9 Make sure you also have a baking tray lined with baking paper ready.

10 Unwrap the balls from their cling film and take each one down the preparation line — flour, egg and breadcrumbs — ensuring that at each stage they are completely coated, with no gaps or bald patches. At the end of the process, you will be looking at four totally breadcrumbed Scotch eggs.

11 Brush generously with the melted butter, then bake in the middle of the oven for 20 minutes, turning them over halfway through to try to maintain their roundness and avoid flat bottoms.

12 Leave to cool for 5 minutes before tucking in — that yolk should still have some glossiness to it and be pretty magnificent to behold!

'AUNT FANNY'S CHICKEN & EGG SALAD

SERVES 5 (of course)

Ingredients

THE MUST-HAVES:

4 eggs
2 heads of baby gem lettuce
1 large carrot, peeled and grated
150g (approx.) cold roast chicken,
   in bite-sized pieces

CHOICE OF TOPPERS:

100g frozen peas, defrosted

150g baby beetroot, sliced/quartered
   (from a jar or vacuum-packed)
1 punnet of mustard cress
12 cherry tomatoes, halved
6—8 English radishes, sliced or
   quartered, if you like them

TO DRESS:

salad cream (or salad dressing of your
choice, e.g. the Balsamic and Poppyseed
Vinaigrette on p108)

Method

1 Fill a small saucepan with water, add a dash of vinegar and bring to a rolling boil. Carefully but quickly lower in the eggs one by one, using a slotted spoon, then reduce the heat to a simmer and cook for 10 minutes exactly.

2 While the eggs are cooking, build the salad. Arrange the lettuce leaves in your chosen dish so they are quite closely packed and then scatter on the grated carrot and peas, if using.

3 Tip the eggs into the sink — water and all — making sure that their shells crack as they land (to make them easier to peel later). Pop the eggs back into their pan and run cold water over them until they are completely cold when you hold one in your hand.

4 When the eggs are ready, peel, quarter and position to your liking on the salad base, then arrange all your other ingredients in simple piles or lines on the leaves.

5 Finish by dressing with zigzags of salad cream (or a dressing of your choice).

JAM SPONGE CAKE

SERVES
8

Ingredients

220g caster sugar + extra for the top
220g unsalted butter, softened + extra for
  greasing
4 large eggs
220g self-raising flour
1 heaped tsp baking powder
½ tsp vanilla extract
2 tbsp milk

FOR THE BUTTERCREAM ICING:

75g unsalted butter, softened
150g icing sugar, sifted
couple of drops of vanilla extract
splash of milk (about ½ tbsp)

FOR THE FILLING:

4—6 tbsp strawberry or raspberry jam

You will need two 20cm sandwich tins.

Method

1 Preheat the oven to 180°C (160°C fan/gas mark 4).

2 Grease and line the base of your sandwich tins with baking paper.

3 Cream together the sugar and softened butter in a large bowl (or use an electric mixer/beater) until pale, light and fluffy. Crack the eggs in one at a time, beating well after each one.

4 Carefully fold in the flour, baking powder and vanilla extract, then finish by stirring in the milk.

5 Divide the mixture evenly between the cake tins.

6 Bake in the oven for 20–25 minutes until the cakes are lovely and light golden brown, well risen and springy to touch – but be careful, they're HOT!

7 Leave to cool in the tin for about 5 minutes and then tip out on to a wire rack, peel off the paper and allow to cool completely.

8 To make the buttercream, beat the butter and sifted icing sugar together using an electric mixer, so it's super-light and pale and creamy, which will take a good few minutes. Then trickle in a drop or two of vanilla and a tiny splash of milk, and briefly beat again.

9 To assemble, take your least favourite of the two sponges and put it, top-side down, on to a cake stand or plate. Using a palette knife, spread the buttercream over the sponge, smearing it right to the edge. Dollop your jam on top and spread it over the butter icing.

10 Gently sit your favourite sponge on top to make the sandwich, then sprinkle with a little caster sugar for a crunchy top.

GORGEOUS GINGER BEER

MAKES 2.5L

Ingredients

fresh ginger (about 15g), unpeeled and finely chopped

1 unwaxed lemon, thickly sliced

300g golden caster sugar

½ tsp cream of tartar

¾ tsp dried fast-action yeast

lemon or lime wedges, to serve

You'll also need enough bottles to store 3 litres of liquid. Used mineral water bottles are easiest, as you don't have to sterilize them — simply keep the lids on once they're empty and rinse just before using. For other bottles, run them through the dishwasher and screw their lids back on as soon as they come out.

NOTE: THIS WILL TAKE SEVERAL DAYS TO BE READY TO DRINK.

Method

1 Put all of the ingredients except the yeast into a large pan over a medium heat, along with 750ml of cold water.

2 Slowly bring to the boil, stirring all the time until all the sugar is dissolved, then reduce the heat and simmer for 5 minutes.

3 Turn the heat off, add 1½ litres of cold water, sprinkle the yeast on top, cover with a lid and put in a cool place overnight.

4 The next day, strain the entire contents of the pan through a sieve into a big bowl. Then pour through a funnel to divide the liquid between the bottles, leaving a good four-finger gap at the top to allow for the build-up of gas that comes during the fermentation process — this is what makes our ginger beer fizzy!

5 Screw the lids on tightly and put back in the cool place for a second night.

6 The next morning, carefully unscrew the lids a bit to check if there has been any build-up of gas. Don't be miffed if nothing has happened yet — depending on the yeast, time of year and temperature of your chosen spot, it'll probably take 3—5 days to get fizzy, but just in case check it every 24 hours.

7 When you hear that satisfying fizz as you unscrew the lid, you can move the bottles into the fridge ready to drink. From this point, you've got about 3 or 4 days before it starts to taste a bit old and yeasty, but I'd be surprised if it hung around that long, especially when poured over ice with a piece of lemon or, even better, lime.

Teatime Treats
up the
Faraway
Tree

Up to the Land of Goodies

Dear Joe, Beth, Frannie and Rick,

The Land of Goodies is here and goes tomorrow.
We have waited and waited for you to come.
If you don't come tomorrow we shall have to go by
ourselves. Can't you come?

Love from,
Silky, Saucepan and Moon-Face

The children talked together, excited.

'I won't have any breakfast,' said Beth. 'It's not much good
going to the Land of Goodies unless we're hungry!'

'That's a good idea,' said Rick. 'I think I won't have any
supper tonight either!'

So when the time came for the four children to set off to the Enchanted Wood, they were terribly hungry!

They ran to the Faraway Tree and climbed up it in excitement.

'I hope there are doughnuts,' said Joe.

'I want chocolate mousse,' said Beth.

'I can't begin to say the things I'd like,' said greedy Rick.

'Well, don't,' said Joe. 'Save your breath and hurry. You're being left behind!'

They got to Moon-Face's, and shouted loudly to him. He came running out of his tree-house in delight.

'Oh, good, good!' he cried. 'You are nice and early. Silky, they're here! Go down and call old Saucepan. He's with Mister Watzisname. I'm sure Saucepan would like to come too.' It wasn't long before seven excited people were climbing up the ladder to the Land of Goodies. How they longed to see what it was like!

Well, it was much better than anyone imagined! It was a small place, set with little crooked houses and shops – and every house and shop was made from things to eat! The first house that the children saw was amazing.

'Look at that house!' cried Joe. 'Its walls are made of sugar – and the chimneys are chocolate – and the window sills are peppermint cream!'

'And look at that shop!' cried Rick. 'It's got walls made of chocolate, and the door is made of marzipan. And I'm sure the windowsills are gingerbread!'

The Land of Goodies was really a very extraordinary place. Everything in it seemed to be eatable. And then the children caught sight of the trees and bushes and called out in surprise:

'Look! That tree is growing muffins!'

'And that one has got buds that are opening out into cakes! It's a cake tree!'

'And look at this little tree here – it's growing big, flat, white flowers like plates – and the middle of the flowers is full of ice-cream. Let's taste it.'

They tasted it – and it was ice-cream!

There was another small bush that grew clusters of a curious-looking fruit, like flat berries of all colours – and, will you believe it, when the children picked the fruit it was really little lollipops, all neatly growing together like a bunch of grapes. 'Ooh, lovely!' said Joe, who liked lollipops very much. 'Gosh, look at that white fence over there – surely it isn't made of marshmallow!'

It was. The children tore off pieces from the fence, and munched the marshmallow. It was the nicest they had ever tasted.

The shops were full of things to eat. You should have seen them! Joe felt as if he would like a hot dog and he went into a hot dog shop. The rolls were tumbling one by one out of a machine.

The handle was being turned by an odd-looking person. He was flat and golden brown, and had raisin-like eyes.

'I think he is a gingerbread man!' whispered Joe to the others. 'He's just like the gingerbread people that Mother makes for us.'

The children chose a hot dog each and went out, munching.

from *The Magic Faraway Tree*
by *Enid Blyton*

GOOGLE BUNS

MAKES
8

Ingredients

FOR THE BUNS:

50ml double cream

80ml full-fat milk

200g plain flour + extra for dusting

40g caster sugar

20g butter, softened + extra for greasing

1 egg

5g dried active yeast

¼ tsp salt

30g currants

1 egg yolk, beaten with 1 tbsp milk
('eggwash')

TO DECORATE:

120g icing sugar

1½ tbsp lemon juice

Method

1 Pour the cream and milk into a small saucepan and gently warm through. Do not let it boil.

2 Tip all the other ingredients for the buns — except the eggwash — into the bowl of a stand mixer with a dough hook, making sure that the yeast and the salt are on opposite sides of the bowl — not in contact with each other at all.

3 Mix gently for a few minutes until it has come together roughly.

4 Gently pour in the warmed cream and milk and when it's incorporated, turn the speed on the mixer up to high for 3–4 minutes until the sides of the bowl are quite clean and the dough is making a satisfying slapping sound!

5 Grease a large baking tray (the biggest that will fit in your oven) with a little bit of butter.

6 Scatter a handful of flour on your work surface. Tip the super-floppy wet dough out, give it a quick knead, then use the flats of your palms to roll it into an even-ish log shape, roughly 30cm long.

7 Cut the log in half widthways, then in half again, and finally cut each bit in half again to end up with eight even pieces. Chuck each one on to the scales quickly — you want them to be roughly 60g each, give or take a few grams.

8 Take one piece of dough and, using the flat of your palm, roll it first into a smooth ball (with no creases on the top), then into a tapered fat sausage about 10cm long.

9 Put it gently on the baking tray and get on with the rest. Space them in two rows about 3—4cm apart so they can puff up as they prove (rise) and cook.

10 Drape a clean tea towel over them and put somewhere warm (the airing cupboard is ideal, but near a warm stove is good too) for 1—1½ hours. The dough is ready when you gently prod it and it springs back to fill in the hole left by your fingertip.

11 Preheat the oven to 190°C (170°C fan/gas mark 5) and whisk up the egg yolk and milk with a fork for the eggwash.

12 Generously brush eggwash all over the buns-to-be, then bake in the middle of the oven for 10—12 minutes until they are golden on the top and bottom (use a tea towel/grown-up to pick one up to check!)

13 Cool for about 5 minutes, then move them on to a wire rack sitting on top of the tray you baked them on.

14 Sift the icing sugar into a bowl. Very carefully measure in the lemon juice — too much and it'll be too runny — and stir until smooth.

15 When the buns are completely cool, spoon on the dribbly icing and, if the mood takes you, draw on some googly eyes in black squeezy writing icing.

MOTHER'S MACAROONS

Ingredients

MAKES 24

175g desiccated coconut
165g caster sugar
1 egg, beaten
80ml evaporated milk

3 tbsp self-raising flour
knob of butter, for greasing
100g chocolate, for the tops (dark, milk or
  white ... your choice ... you can even do a
  two-tone combo)

Method

1 In a mixing bowl, stir together the coconut, sugar, beaten egg and evaporated milk.

2 Add the flour and mix well to make sure there are no lumps.

3 Put in the fridge for 1 hour to soften the coconut (not essential though, if you're in a hurry — skipping this step just makes for a slightly chewier macaroon ... good jaw workout!)

4 Line a large baking tray or two small ones with baking paper, and then rub lightly with butter.

5 Wet the palms of your hands, then take a small handful of the mix and roll it into a walnut-sized ball. Repeat until you have 24 balls.

6 Put them on the tray(s) slightly spaced apart, then bake at 160°C (140°C/gas mark 3) for 10–15 minutes until golden and just beginning to go a bit brown and crunchy on top.

7 Take out of the oven and place on a wire rack to cool. Slide the baking paper you cooked them on underneath the rack to catch the chocolate drips later.

8 Meanwhile, pour roughly 5cm of water into a small saucepan, bring to the boil, then lower the heat to a very gentle simmer. Break your chosen chocolate up into squares and put it in a heatproof bowl that sits snugly on top of the steaming saucepan — making sure that the bottom of the bowl doesn't touch the water.

9 Stir the chocolate with a spatula until it's mostly melted but lift it off the saucepan while there are still one or two small chunks — the residual heat should melt them.

10 Put a dinner plate on to a sheet of baking paper, draw around it and cut out the circle.

11 Fold the circle in half four times, then stick your finger inside to make a pocket in the cone. Pour or spoon the melted chocolate into the cone.

12 Cut the very end off the paper cone (watch out for instantly dribbling chocolate), then squiggle madly all over the now-cooled macaroons.

13 When the chocolate has set, store the macaroons in an airtight container — good for about 3—4 days.

SILKY'S POP CAKES

Ingredients

FOR THE HONEY 'POP' INSIDES:

95g white chocolate
65g unsalted butter
125g honey
3 tbsp water

FOR THE CAKEY OUTSIDES:

225g unsalted butter, softened + extra for greasing
200g golden caster sugar

2 eggs
125g ground almonds
¼ tsp baking powder
1 lemon
350g plain flour + extra for your palms
salt

Plus some popping candy, sugar nibs, edible glitter etc. to decorate for extra **POP!**

You will need a 12-hole deep muffin tray.

The honey 'pop' insides need to be made a couple of hours in advance (or the day before).

Method

1 First make the honey insides. Break the white chocolate into pieces and chuck in a mixing bowl. Chop the butter into similar size chunks and put into the bowl too.

2 In a small pan, bring the honey and water to the boil and let it bubble for 2–3 minutes, making sure it doesn't boil over.

3 Pour the honey mixture over the butter and chocolate. Mix quickly with a rubber spatula until smooth and everything has melted.

4 Leave to set in the fridge for a couple of hours (or make it the day before).

5 Preheat the oven to 180°C (160°C/gas mark 4) and grease your muffin tray with butter. Now you can make the cakey outside …

6 Using an electric whisk or upright stand mixer, cream together the butter and the sugar until light and fluffy.

7 Add the eggs one at a time, beating after each one until smooth, then take the bowl off the mixer, if using.

8 Tip in the ground almonds, baking powder, a pinch of salt, and the zest (finely grated peel) from the lemon. Now using a wooden spoon, stir well until combined.

9 Finally, sieve in the flour in three or four stages until the dough comes together and is completely smooth.

10 Lightly flour the palms of your hands and divide the dough into two uneven batches, roughly one-third, and two-thirds. Using the larger batch of dough, make 12 large (approx. 60g) balls, rolling between your palms. Using the smaller batch of dough, make 12 smaller (approx. 25g) balls. Put the smaller balls into the fridge.

11 Take the 12 larger balls, flatten each one slightly and pop one in each muffin tin hole. Push the dough disc into the base and up the sides evenly to line it, creating a well. Now use your thumb to make a thicker ledge at the top that you can rest the lid on when the cakes are filled.

12 Take the honey-caramel from the fridge — it should be quite thick but still spoonable. Using a teaspoon, put a dollop in each hole. Don't be tempted to overfill them as it will just bubble out when they are cooking. If you've done your portioning right, you should have a little left over — put this aside for later.

13 Take the 12 smaller balls out of the fridge. Lightly flour your palms again and flatten each ball slightly to make thick circles. Use these as lids to cover and seal the cakes, so the insides can't leak out. The lids should be flat, not domed, so they look a bit like mince pies. Make sure you smooth the seam with your fingertips so you can't see the join.

14 Bake in the oven for 15–20 minutes until golden, then leave them to cool slightly before lifting them onto a wire rack.

15 When completely cool, warm the remainder of the honey-caramel and drizzle over the cakes. Top each one with a sprinkling of popping candy (or your chosen decoration) for extra pop!

TOFFEE FOR MOON-FACE

Ingredients

200g caster sugar

100g dark soft brown sugar

200g golden syrup

150g unsalted butter, cut into cubes

200ml double cream

125ml evaporated milk

1 tsp vanilla extract

You will need a sugar thermometer, long sleeves to protect your arms and, if you're feeling extra-cautious, gloves (NOT rubber)!

Method

1 Line a large baking tray (about 30cm x 40cm) with baking paper.

2 Your choice of saucepan is pretty crucial to Operation Safe Toffee. My toffee-making pan is 25cm across, 12cm deep with a thick-ish bottom ... and I suggest you find something similar. It needs to be high because the toffee will be bubbling and simmering and you don't want it to get too near the top of the pan. The thick bottom is to spread the heat better so that it doesn't catch and burn in one spot.

3 Pour all the ingredients except the vanilla extract into your chosen pan.

4 Over a medium–high heat, stir constantly until all the sugar has dissolved, the butter is melted and the whole mix is smooth.

5 Turn the heat up to full and remember, from here until it's done, never lower the heat again, not even for a second. The Toffee-Making Miracle happens at full pelt heat-wise, but it's not instant — you'll be at the hob solidly for about the next 20–25 minutes.

6 First, the toffee will rise slightly and start to bubble and, as it goes over 100°C, it really starts to look like caramel lava. From here till the finish line, whisk gently but continuously. Make sure you sweep the bottom of the pan with every whisk as, at these temperatures, sugar burns very easily, and you'll find that, once one part is burnt, it will contaminate the whole batch.

7 Hold your nerve (easier said than done) until it reaches the hard ball stage, when it's a shade shy of 130°C, then turn off the heat but don't relax yet! Keep whisking as you tip in the vanilla extract, making it bubble up, then immediately pour the toffee on to the prepared baking tray.

8 Hold the tray just around the edges and tip it so that the toffee is more or less of an even thickness across the whole tray, then leave to cool completely. This will take longer than you think — certainly a couple of hours and as many as six if it's a warm day.

9 When it's cold, just whack the toffee with a hammer/ rolling pin to break it up into pieces. Lasts for weeks in an open container — gets a bit sweaty and sticky in an airtight one.

CLEMENTINE TREACLE TART

SERVES 8

it's super-sweet!

Ingredients

1 pack (about 300g) ready-made sweet
  shortcrust pastry (or make your own — see right)
  + plain flour, for dusting
1 egg
200g white bread, crusts off
6 clementines (or 2 large/3 small oranges)
500g golden syrup
juice of 1 lemon
1 tbsp milk
double cream, to serve

IF YOU WANT TO MAKE YOUR OWN PASTRY:

170g plain flour + extra for dusting
60g icing sugar
120g unsalted butter, cold and cut into 8
  cubes
1 egg

You will need a pie dish, approximately
24cm across and 5cm deep, either a
slope-sided metal or china pie dish, or
a fluted tart tin with a push-up bottom.

Method

TO MAKE YOUR OWN PASTRY:

1 Put the flour and icing sugar into the food processor
and whizz for a few seconds, then leave it whizzing while
you quickly drop the butter cubes in one by one. As soon
as the last one is incorporated turn it off — it should have
been whirring for less than 30 seconds in total.

2 Crack in the egg and spin for a final count of 5.

3 The pastry dough should more or less be in a ball. Use
a rubber spatula to scrape it into a piece of cling film, wrap
it up and stick it in the fridge for 30 minutes or freezer for
15 minutes to have a bit of a rest.

TO MAKE THE TART:

1 Preheat the oven to 190°C (170°C fan/gas mark 5).

2 Scatter a handful of flour on your work surface and
roll out your homemade or ready-made pastry until it's
about 0.5cm thick.

3 Lay it into your chosen dish, pushing it into the base
and up the sides well with your fingertips. Pressing round
the edge with the tines of the a fork is a simple, classic
way to finish a pie edge, but if you're using a tart tin
without a border, then it's easiest to just roll over the top
with a rolling pin, thus cutting off the excess.

4 Use the offcuts for plugging any cracks you spot after the blind-baking stage to follow. If you have any left over after that, you could stick it in the freezer for next time — pastry lasts for ages in the freezer.

5 When your tart case is beautifully lined, pop it back in the fridge to firm up again for about 30 minutes (or if you're in a hurry, in the freezer for 15 minutes).

6 When it's firm, line the pastry case with baking paper, fill it with baking beans and put it on the bottom shelf of the oven to bake for 10–12 minutes.

7 Take it out of the oven, carefully lift out the baking paper and beans and set them aside. Turn the pastry case round 180° so it colours evenly, and pop it back in the oven.

8 Cook for 5 more minutes. While it is cooking, separate the egg, putting the yolk and white into separate mugs. Whip the white with a fork until loose and frothy.

9 Take the tart out of the oven, give it a thorough brush with the beaten egg white and put it back in for 5 more minutes so this glaze can set hard and shiny. All of this in-and-out of the oven is to stop the tart having a soggy bottom — what a letdown that would be!

10 Meanwhile, put the crustless bread into a food processor and whizz briefly to make fluffy breadcrumbs.

11 Zest (finely grate the peel) the clementines (or oranges) using the small holes on a grater, a microplane or a zester if you have one.

12 In a medium saucepan on a low heat, stir the breadcrumbs, zest and golden syrup as it warms through and becomes runny and combined. Do not let it boil.

13 Turn the heat off, cool slightly, then stir in the juice from the clementines (or oranges) and lemon.

14 Take the egg yolk you've set aside, add the milk, and briefly whisk with a fork to make your eggwash.

15 Pour the filling into the prepared pastry case, brush the eggwash around the edge of the pastry, then bake in the bottom half of the oven for about 30 minutes — give or take a few mins depending on your oven — until puffed up and perfect.

16 Resist temptation and that enticing aroma and leave to cool until almost room temperature, before tucking in — hot syrup can scald! Dreamy with a bit of double cream.

RASPBERRY & VANILLA WATER-ICE

SERVES 8 KIDS

enough for an elf party!

Ingredients

450g raspberries
about 100g icing sugar, to taste, depending
  on the tartness of the fruit
juice of ½ lemon
½ tsp vanilla extract

You can make this with any fruit — particularly satisfying and tasty with homegrown or pick-your-own.

Keeps for a few months in the freezer with a tight lid — in the depths of winter it's uplifting to remind yourself what the English summer tastes like.

Method

1 Put the raspberries, most of the sugar and the lemon juice into an upright blender. Add an eggcupful of water and whizz until puréed.

2 Pour into a sieve over a bowl and take a good 5 minutes to press the juice through the sieve, using the back of a spoon, until all you have is a load of pips in the sieve.

3 Pour another eggcupful of water over the pips and give them a quick stir to wash through any remaining flavour clinging to them.

4 Measure the vanilla extract into the smooth juice and taste. Fruit has different levels of sweetness depending on variety and time of year, so you may need to add more icing sugar or lemon juice to suit your tastes — just bear in mind that it will get a good notch less sweet as it freezes.

5 Pour into a plastic box with a lid or lolly moulds and stick in the freezer.

6 If you've gone for the box option and you're planning to eat it later the same day, you'll need to stir it every hour and it'll take a few hours to set (and if you're in a real hurry the thinner the layer the quicker it'll set, so pour it into a small baking tray if it'll fit in your freezer).

7 If you're going to eat it another day, however, there's no need to stir, just let it set solid overnight. Take it out of the freezer ahead of time: it'll be spoonable after 30—45 minutes at room temperature. (Lollies don't need stirring at all of course!)

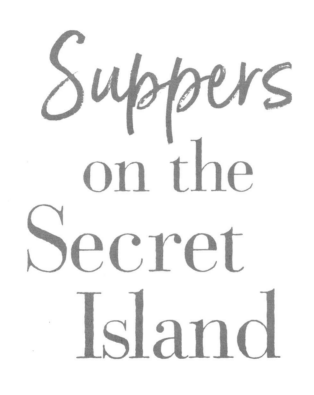

Suppers
on the
Secret
Island

A Secret Island Supper

After breakfast the four of them set to work to make a tiny yard for the hens. They used willow stakes again and quickly built a fine little fence, too high for the hens to jump over. Jack made them nesting places of bracken, and hoped they would lay their eggs there. He scattered some seed for them, and they pecked at it eagerly. Peggy gave them a dish of water.

'They will soon know this is their home and lay their eggs here,' said Jack. 'Now, come on, let's get on with Willow House! You two girls stuff up the cracks with heather and bracken, and Mike and I will make the door.'

Everyone worked hard. The girls found it rather a nice job to stuff the soft heather and bracken into the cracks and make the house rain and windproof. They were so happy in their job that they did not notice what a fine door Jack and Mike had made of woven willow twigs. The boys called the girls, and proudly showed them what they had done.

The door had even been fixed on some sort of a hinge, so that it swung open and shut! It looked fine! It did not quite fit at the top, but nobody minded that. It was a door – and could be shut or opened, just as they pleased. Willow House was very dark inside when the door was shut – but that made it all the more exciting!

'I'm so hungry and thirsty now that I believe I could eat all the food we've got!' said Mike at last.

'Yes, we really must have something to eat,' said Jack. 'We've got plenty of bread and potatoes and vegetables. Let's cook some broad beans. They are jolly good. Go and look at my fishing line, Mike, and see if there are any fish on it.'

There was a fine trout, and Mike brought it back to cook. Soon the smell of frying rose on the air, and the children sniffed hungrily. Fish, potatoes, bread, beans, cherries and cocoa with milk from one of Jack's tins. What a meal!

'I'll think about getting Daisy the cow across next,' said Jack, drinking his cocoa. 'We simply must have milk.'

'And, Jack, we could store some of our things in Willow

House now, couldn't we?' said Peggy. 'The ants get into some of the things in the cave-larder. It's a good place for things like hammers and nails, but it would be better to keep our food in Willow House. Are we going to live in Willow House, Jack?'

'Well, we'll live in the open air mostly, I expect,' said Jack, 'but it will be a good place to sleep in when the nights are cold and rainy, and a good shelter on bad days. It's our sort of home.'

'It's a lovely home,' said Nora. The nicest there ever was! What fun it is to live like this!'

from *The Secret Island*
by Enid Blyton

CREAMY PEA KEDGEREE

Ingredients

300g 'easy cook' long-grain rice
2 tbsp butter
1 tbsp vegetable or sunflower oil
1 large or 2 small white onions (about 350g),
  chopped
2 tsp mild curry powder
½ tsp turmeric
2 tsp vegetable bouillon powder
  or 1 vegetable stock cube

dash of vinegar (any will do)
4 eggs
100g peas (defrosted if frozen)
30g sultanas or currants
200g undyed smoked mackerel, skinned,
  flaked and checked for bones
100ml double cream
1 tsp salt
pepper

SERVES 4-6

+ leftovers for brekkie tomorrow

Kedgeree recipes are over 100 years old, coming from colonial India — hence the curry powder. At the time it was mostly eaten at breakfast — that'll wake you up!

Method

1 First, put the rice into a sieve and run cold water over it for a couple of minutes, moving it around with a spoon or your hand until the water runs clear, not cloudy (you're washing the starch off here to stop the rice being sticky when it's cooked).

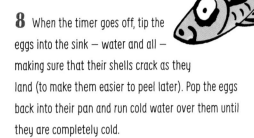

2 In a saucepan at least 20cm across and 10cm deep, melt the butter in the oil over a medium—high heat. As it starts to sizzle, tip in the chopped onion.

3 Stir it from time to time, until you can see the onion losing its bright whiteness and softening — about 5 minutes — then stir in the curry powder, turmeric and vegetable bouillon powder (or crumbled stock cube).

4 Turn the heat down to medium low and give it all a really good mix for another couple of minutes, keeping it on the move so it doesn't stick to the bottom of the pan.

5 Tip in the washed and drained rice and coat it well in the onions and spices. Then pour in enough cold water to cover the rice by 3cm (use your ruler/a grown-up — it's important to get this measurement right!). You will need about 700ml of water, depending on the size of your pan.

6 Turn the heat up and bring the water to the boil, then turn it down to the lowest setting, put on a well-fitting lid and don't lift it for a peek for 15 minutes.

7 Meanwhile, put the eggs in a pan, cover with cold water, add a dash of vinegar and bring to the boil. When it hits a busy rolling boil, turn the heat off and set your timer for 6 minutes (or 7 minutes if you've got large eggs, which I don't tend to use).

8 When the timer goes off, tip the eggs into the sink — water and all — making sure that their shells crack as they land (to make them easier to peel later). Pop the eggs back into their pan and run cold water over them until they are completely cold.

9 Peel them very gently — try to break the membrane under the shell for an easier job. They are somewhere between soft and hard-boiled, with a hard white but runny yolk. This is how I like them on my kedgeree but if you prefer a fully hard-boiled egg, boil them for 9 minutes instead. Pop the peeled eggs in a small heatproof bowl.

10 When the rice has had 15 minutes, lift up the lid but do not stir. Stick a teaspoon in and lift out a few grains of rice, blow on them furiously and then gingerly taste — they should be pretty much cooked, but if they've still got a bit of crunch, then put the lid back on and try again in 5 minutes.

11 When you think the rice is just about cooked, the Do Not Stir Rule still applies. Turn the heat off, scatter the surface of the rice with the peas and sultanas/currants and put the lid back on, so it steams a bit longer and warms the rest of the ingredients.

12 Boil the kettle and pour water over the eggs to warm them through for a couple of minutes, then drain.

13 After 5 minutes' steaming time, take the lid off the rice, chuck in the flaked smoked mackerel, double cream and salt, then give it all a Jolly Good Stir.

14 Serve up your kedgeree with pride ... and halved eggs on top!

JACK'S TROUT
with fried almonds and lemony-butter sauce

SERVES
4

Ingredients

50g salted butter + a few extra knobs for
   the fish
30g flaked almonds
2 lemons

4 portion-sized trout (350–400g each),
   scaled and gutted (the fishmonger will do this)
few sprigs of fresh herbs (such as thyme,
   parsley or oregano)
2 tbsp olive oil
salt and black pepper

Method

1 Choose whether you want to cook the fish under
the grill (easier) or on a griddle pan (which I slightly
prefer), or even on a barbecue, for a proper outdoor-
adventure taste. Whichever you choose, preheat
your heat source to very hot. If you've gone for
a griddle, you'll also need to preheat the oven
to 200°C (180°C fan/gas mark 6), as you'll
probably only be able to fit two whole fish
in your pan at a time.

2 Melt the butter in a standard frying pan
and, as it starts to sizzle and froth, tip in the
flaked almonds and a pinch of salt.

3 Stirring pretty much constantly (as nuts can burn very
easily), cook for 3–4 minutes until they are an all-over
gorgeous golden-brown, then turn off the heat. Squeeze in
the juice of half a lemon and grind in a bit of black pepper.

4 With the almond butter made and the grill/griddle
now roasting hot, season the fish inside and out. Cut a
whole lemon into slices and put a few inside the fish,
along with a couple of knobs of butter and a few sprigs of
fresh herbs.

5 For grilling: line the grill tray with foil and lightly
brush with oil. Lay all four fish down, season with salt, and
grill for 4–6 minutes per side, depending on the strength
of your grill and the size of the fish. Check they are cooked
by inserting a thin knife into the thickest part of the flesh,
just behind the head, until it hits the bone. Leave it here
for a count of 3, then remove it and quickly touch it to
your top lip: if it's cold, pop the fish back under the grill for
another couple of minutes; if it's hot, get noshing; and if
it's warm, well, it could go either way — it depends how
well you like your fish cooked.

6 For griddling: lightly oil the outside of the fish and season with salt. Lay two fish at a time on the griddle. After about 4 minutes, gingerly try to lift one of them — it's ready to be turned if the skin comes away from the griddle and does not tear.

7 Cook for a similar time on the other side and do the cooked test with the knife as for the grill method.

8 Serve up the fish — one each — with the remaining half-lemon cut into four wedges, rice or potatoes and some kind of green veg.

9 Lastly, have a quick taste of the nutty butter for salt, pepper and lemony-ness, then spoon copiously all over the frazzled fishies.

SAUSAGE & BEAN CASSEROLE

SERVES 6

Ingredients

1 large onion, peeled and chopped

1 large carrot, cut into small chunks

2 garlic cloves, peeled and finely chopped

1 red pepper, deseeded and cut into chunks

1 tbsp butter

1 tbsp sunflower or vegetable oil

350g cocktail sausages (or big ones cut into 4)

1 tin (230g) kidney beans* drained and rinsed

1 tin (230g) haricot beans* drained and rinsed

3 tbsp tomato purée

1 tin (400g) chopped tomatoes

2 tbsp BBQ sauce

0.5 litre chicken stock (better from concentrated tub, not cube)

1 tsp salt

*or any other beans you have/like

This is a great complete meal, with all food groups (well, it's a bit light on veg but there is some in there ... corn on the side would be in keeping). Plenty of protein and carbs make for a nice full tummy, a good night's sleep and waking up sprightly!

Method

1 First, chop the onion, carrot, garlic and red pepper so they are ready when you need them.

2 In a medium-sized ovenproof saucepan or casserole dish, melt the butter in the oil over a high heat. When melted and hot, fry the sausages for 4–5 minutes, turning now and then until nicely browned.

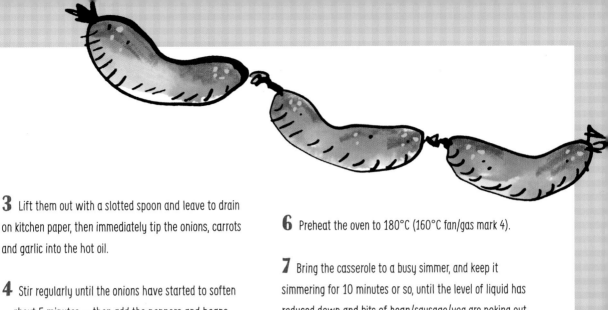

3 Lift them out with a slotted spoon and leave to drain on kitchen paper, then immediately tip the onions, carrots and garlic into the hot oil.

4 Stir regularly until the onions have started to soften — about 5 minutes — then add the peppers and beans. Keeping the heat quite high, mix everything together well and when it's all properly hot, squeeze in the tomato purée.

5 Give it all a really good stir to coat in the tomato purée for 2–3 minutes, then tip the sausages back in, along with the tin of tomatoes, BBQ sauce, chicken stock and salt.

6 Preheat the oven to 180°C (160°C fan/gas mark 4).

7 Bring the casserole to a busy simmer, and keep it simmering for 10 minutes or so, until the level of liquid has reduced down and bits of bean/sausage/veg are poking out the top. Remember to stir it every now and then, to make sure it's not sticking anywhere on the bottom.

8 Pop a lid on and put it in the oven for 40 minutes, then take it out and leave to rest for 10 minutes before tucking in. Great with crusty bread and corn on the cob!

SMASHING POTATO SALAD

Ingredients

600g new potatoes (the smaller the better)
3-4 tbsp mayonnaise
dash of wholegrain, Dijon or American
  mustard, if you fancy
squeeze of lemon juice

drizzle of olive or vegetable oil
small handful of fresh parsley, chopped
2 spring onions, roughly chopped
4 radishes, thinly sliced
1 celery stick, sliced
salt and pepper

Method

1 Bring a large saucepan of salted water to the boil. The pan needs to be big enough for the potatoes to be submerged. When it's boiling, carefully drop in the spuds, reduce the heat and simmer for 12–15 minutes until tender.

2 Drain the potatoes and leave in the colander to steam-dry.

3 While the potatoes are cooling, make the dressing. Spoon the mayonnaise into a large bowl. Stir in your favourite mustard (if using), a good squeeze of lemon juice, a drizzle of oil and some freshly chopped parsley. Taste and season with salt and pepper.

4 Tip the spuds back into the pan, then gently 'smash' them, using a fork or masher, so they're lightly crushed — a cross between whole potatoes and mash. Then topple them into the dressing bowl, add the spring onions, radishes and celery and give it all a Jolly Good Mix to coat.

5 Have a little taste to see if it needs more salt and pepper but try not to scoff the lot as it is totally smashingly scrummy!

STRAWBERRY, MINT & SPINACH SALAD

with balsamic and poppyseed dressing

Ingredients

SERVES 4

FOR THE SALAD:

50g pine nuts

150g baby spinach

½ cucumber, cut into chunks

1 ripe avocado, roughly chopped

220g strawberries, hulled and halved/
  quartered, depending on size

2 handfuls of small mint leaves
  — I prefer whole but chop if you want

FOR THE DRESSING:

1½ tbsp balsamic vinegar (or try with
  raspberry vinegar if you can find it)

½ tbsp lemon juice

½ tbsp poppy seeds

2 tbsp olive oil (not extra virgin — too
  strong)

1 tsp honey

pinch of salt

Method

1 Set the oven to 180°C (160°C fan/gas mark 4), spread the pine nuts out on a small baking tray or ovenproof frying pan and pop them in the oven immediately, while it is coming up to temperature.

2 Knock up the dressing by putting all the ingredients into a jam jar, screwing the lid on tight and giving it a good old shake.

3 Give the pine nuts a quick shuffle after 5 minutes, so they colour evenly. Roughly speaking, by the time the oven is up to temperature (10–12 minutes), the pine nuts should be golden brown. Then you can turn the oven off.

4 While the pine nuts are toasting, get on with your salad construction. I'd do this one in layers: spinach on the bottom, then cucumber, avocado, strawberries, mint and lastly the pine nuts.

5 Once folks have seen quite how beautiful your salad is, give the dressing another shake, then pour it all over and toss lightly so all the leaves are coated.

MELT-IN-THE-MOUTH MERINGUES

with freshly picked berries and cream

Ingredients

FOR THE MERINGUE:

2 egg whites
100g caster sugar

MERINGUE FLAVOURING IDEAS:

Take your pick — don't do all of them together!

finely grated zest (peel) of 1 lemon or orange
OR handful of your favourite nuts (such as
hazelnuts or pistachios), roughly chopped
OR 1 tbsp cocoa, sifted

FOR THE CREAM:

175ml double cream
2 tbsp icing sugar, sifted
1 orange
few drops of vanilla extract

TO SERVE:

small handful of freshly picked berries, such
as raspberries, blackberries, strawberries,
cut into halves or quarters
icing sugar, to dust

Method

1 Preheat the oven to 140°C (120°C
fan/gas mark 1) and line a large baking
sheet with baking paper.

2 Tip the egg whites into a large, spotlessly clean bowl or in the bottom of a free-standing electric mixer. Using an electric whisk, whisk the whites for several minutes until they are frothy and have reached the soft peak stage.

3 Gradually add the sugar a tablespoon or two at a time and continue to whisk until the mixture reaches stiff glossy peaks. To check if it's ready, you can turn the bowl upside down — if it doesn't fall out, it's ready!

4 Carefully fold your favourite flavourings into the meringue mix, swirling to lightly incorporate. If using the cocoa, gently fold it through so it gives a rippled and marbled effect. (You can always divide the meringue mix into batches and have a variety of flavourings.)

5 Dollop the meringue on to the prepared baking sheet in six generous piles, making sure you create some height and characterful shapes along the way. Keep about 3cm space between the piles as they will spread a little while baking.

6 Bake for approximately 1 hour, at which point the plain meringues should be brilliantly white, crisp and easy to remove from the paper without sticking. After a couple of minutes cooling on the paper, move them on to a wire rack to cool completely.

7 Meanwhile, pour the double cream into a large bowl and add the icing sugar, zest (finely grated peel) from the orange and the vanilla extract. Using an electric whisk, lightly beat until you have soft peaks which just hold their shape.

8 Serve your scrumptious meringues with a good dollop of vanilla cream alongside and a plentiful scattering of berries on top.

9 Lastly, dust with icing sugar and … get in! Chewy, crunchy and melt in the mouth all at once!

HOT APPLE TEA *for autumn*

Ingredients

800ml apple juice, preferably cloudy
1 cinnamon stick

2 matchstick slithers of fresh ginger
1 apple, cored and cut into slices

**SERVES
4-6**

*in little
tumblers*

Method

1 Pour the apple juice into a medium–largish
saucepan set over a low heat. Add the cinnamon
stick and ginger slithers. Slowly warm through,
swirling gently to infuse the flavours and bring up to a
relaxed simmer for about 5 minutes.

2 Turn the heat off, add the apple slices and leave to sit
for a minute.

3 Serve up by ladling into little mugs or tumblers.

Midnight Feasts at Malory Towers

Midnight at Malory Towers

Violet tucked the cat into the front of her dressing-gown and made her way back to the dormitory.

The others were busy setting all the food out on plates in the middle of the floor when she returned, and everyone looked up in alarm as the door opened.

'Oh, it's you, Violet!' said Katie. 'My goodness, what a start you gave me. Where have you been?'

'Never mind that,' said Daffy crossly. 'For heaven's sake, shut the door behind you, quickly, Violet. And someone had better put a couple of pillows along the bottom, where the gap is, then we can put the light on.'

Ivy quickly pulled the pillows from her own bed, arranging them along the bottom of the door, before switching on the light. Then she gave a gasp, as she saw Willow's head poking

out from Violet's dressing-gown.

'Willow!' she cried. 'Oh, Violet, you brought her after all. How marvellous!'

'For goodness sake, keep your voice down!' hissed Daffy, before turning to Violet and saying angrily, 'I told you that you weren't to bring Willow to the feast.'

'Why should I do what you say?' said Violet, tossing her golden curls. 'You aren't head of the form, though you sometimes behave as if you are.'

'No, but it's my feast,' said Daffy. 'And I have the right to say who comes and who doesn't. I've a good mind not to let you share in it, Violet!'

Violet was about to make a sharp retort when Jenny said, 'We can hardly throw Violet out of her own dormitory while we enjoy the feast. Besides, she has provided us with that lovely tin of sweets, as well as that delicious-looking chocolate cake, so it wouldn't be fair not to let her share.'

'Very well,' said Daffy with bad grace. 'But that cat had better not cause any trouble.'

'She will be as good as gold,' said Violet, removing Willow, who was beginning to wriggle, from her dressing-gown and placing her on the bed.

Then the first-formers sat on the floor, in a big circle, and settled down to enjoy their feast.

'Scrumptious!' sighed Maggie, taking a bite of pork pie. 'Simply scrumptious.'

'You know, I normally hate sardines,' said Ivy. 'But for some reason I can eat no end of them at a midnight feast.'

'Well, save some for the rest of us!' laughed Ivy. 'I say, Faith, pass the ginger beer, would you?'

The girls ate hungrily, until all that was left was the chocolate cake, sweets and biscuits.

'Shall I cut the cake?' asked Violet.

'Yes, do,' said Jenny. 'I feel awfully full, but I daresay I shall find room for a slice.'

But it was as Violet finished cutting the cake that Willow, who had behaved very well throughout the feast, sitting on the bed, being fed the occasional tit-bit and watching the proceedings with interest, decided to take a little exercise.

The cat suddenly leapt from the bed, landing right in the middle of the cake and showering Daffy, who had just leaned forward to take a slice, with crumbs, chocolate and cream.

There was a horrified silence, and everyone waited for Violet to throw a tantrum and scold the cat. But, to everyone's

astonishment, she threw back her head and laughed until the tears poured down her cheeks. One by one, the others started to laugh too, for Daffy really did look comical with cream all over her face and crumbs everywhere.

from *Malory Towers: Secrets*
by Enid Blyton

CARROT & ORANGE MUFFINS
with candied carrot

MAKES 12

Ingredients

175g light muscovado sugar

150g self-raising flour

75g wholemeal flour

1 heaped tsp mixed spice, cinnamon and/or ginger (choose your favourite or a combo)

1 heaped tsp baking powder

2 small/1 large carrots (about 150g), peeled and grated

1 orange

2 eggs

200ml whole milk

75ml sunflower oil

FOR THE DECORATION:

½ small carrot, peeled

4 tbsp caster sugar

4 tbsp water

You will need a 12-hole muffin tray and paper muffin cases.

Method

1 Preheat the oven to 200°C (180°C fan/gas mark 6) and line your muffin tray with paper muffin cases.

2 Mix together the sugar, flours, spices and baking powder in a large bowl, then stir in the grated carrot and zest (finely grated peel) from the orange.

3 In a separate bowl, beat the eggs with the milk and sunflower oil. Add this to the dry ingredients and beat together with a wooden spoon until well combined, making a loose mix which just runs off the spoon.

4 Carefully scrape it all into a large jug (if you have one), to make it easier to pour into the muffin cases. Or, just do a careful job with a ladle. Either way, pour the mixture equally into the muffin cases.

5 Bake for 25–30 minutes until the muffins are well risen and dark golden-brown. If they are ready, a thin knife inserted into a muffin should come out clean. Leave to cool for a couple of minutes in the tin before lifting the cases on to a wire rack to cool fully.

6 While the muffins are baking, make the candied carrot decoration. Shave the peeled carrot into long ribbons using a vegetable peeler. Slice the ribbons into strips. Then carefully cut the strips into pieces about 4cm long using a sharp knife — or get a handy grown-up to do this.

7 Heat the caster sugar and water in a medium saucepan for about 5 minutes, stirring occasionally, until the sugar has dissolved. Drop in the carrot strips and cook gently for 5–10 minutes, giving it a stir every now and then, until the syrup is thick and sticky and the carrots are glossy and shiny. Set aside to cool, being extra-careful not to touch as they will be super-hot.

8 When the muffins and carrots are cool, use a fork to decorate the top of your muffins with the candied carrots. The sugar may be crunchy now it's starting to set, which makes for added texture!

STICKY PIGLETS

Ingredients

For 1 piglet, you'll need:
1 cocktail sausage
¼ date (stoned), cut lengthways
½ rasher of streaky bacon
vegetable or sunflower oil, for greasing

Make as many as you need or want!

Method

1 Preheat the oven to 190°C (170°C fan/gas mark 5).

2 Put the sausage and the date next to each other, then wrap the bacon around tightly to bind them together.

3 Grease the bottom of a baking tray with oil and arrange the swaddled piglets on it so they are not touching.

4 Bake for 20–25 minutes, turning them over halfway through.

MARVELLOUS MELON BOATS

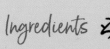

Ingredients

FOR THE BOATS:

½ Galia melon, seeds scraped out with a spoon

½ cantaloupe melon, seeds scraped out with a spoon

handful of mint leaves, chopped

squeeze of lime juice

FOR THE SAILS:

¼ mini watermelon*

8 glacé cherries (or red or green grapes)

You will need 8 small wooden skewers.

* Option: You can make alternative 'sails' from orange or cucumber slices instead of watermelon triangles, if you prefer.

Method

1 Cut the Galia and cantaloupe melon halves into four wedges each, to make eight boats in total. Very carefully, using a sharp knife, cut between the flesh and the skin all the way along the wedge so the flesh is detached.

2 Cut the wedges into four or five chunks of melon. Repeat this with all the wedges, then position back into the 'boats', alternating any colours of melon as you wish.

3 Cut your watermelon into eight small triangles to make your sails. Pop out any of the big seeds as you go. You'll have some left over so snack on this as you're assembling your boats! Carefully guide your 'sail' on to the wooden mast, using scissors to trim the length of the skewer if necessary, then pop a glacé cherry on top to decorate.

4 Arrange your marvellous melon flotilla on serving plates and scatter with chopped mint. Squeeze over a little fresh lime juice for a bit of zing and tuck into the tasty, refreshing treat.

MELTY SWIRLY-WHIRLS

Ingredients

250g unsalted butter, softened, cut into
   small pieces
80g icing sugar
1 tsp vanilla extract

225g plain flour
25g cornflour
250g milk or dark chocolate, for dipping

You will need a piping bag with a 1cm star
nozzle.

These are so called not just because they are dipped in melted chocolate, but also because the biscuits themselves melt in your mouth — heavenly, like Cupid's clouds!

Method

1 Preheat the oven to 165°C (140°C fan/gas mark 3) and line a big baking tray with baking paper.

2 In order to make these light and fluffy, we need the help of electric beaters, so put the butter, icing sugar and vanilla extract into a suitable bowl, either that of an upright mixer or one deep enough for a hand-held mixer.

3 Start the mixing on a slow speed — if you kick off too fast the icing sugar will fly everywhere like a sweet-tasting cloud!

4 Once the icing sugar is mixed with the butter, crank the speed up to full whack for 3 minutes of hard beating until pale and airy.

5 Sieve the flour and cornflour into a bowl. Lower the mixer speed a bit and add the flours into the mix in two stages.

6 Prepare your piping bag with a star nozzle about 1cm across and transfer the mix to the bag, keeping as much air in it as possible — don't squish it down.

7 Pipe out the biscuits in a swirl about 3cm wide, with a nice flick of the wrist at the top to give the break-off a clean finish. Space them roughly a thumb's width apart as they'll spread a bit in the oven.

8 Bake for about 12–14 minutes until golden, then take out and cool on the tray for about 5 minutes before gently lifting on to a wire rack and leaving to cool completely. Put the tray and baking paper to one side for later.

9 Meanwhile, pour roughly 5cm of water into a small saucepan, bring to the boil, then lower the heat to a very gentle simmer. Break the chocolate up into squares and put it in a heatproof bowl that sits snugly on top of the steaming saucepan, making sure that the bottom of the bowl doesn't touch the water.

10 Stir the chocolate with a spatula until it's mostly melted but lift it off the saucepan while there are still one or two small chunks — the residual heat should melt them. The chocolate should feel just warm, not hot, when you put your (clean) fingertip into it (yum). If you've overheated the chocolate, put it in the fridge for a few minutes to bring it back to lukewarm.

11 When the biscuits are cooled and the melted chocolate is at the right temperature, ever so gently pick up a biscuit and dip half of it into the chocolate. Give it a tap to let the excess drip off, then pop it back flat on the baking paper. Repeat with the rest.

12 Leave the biscuits to rest until the chocolate is set firm. Don't be tempted to put them in the fridge to speed it up, as then the chocolate might develop some white-ish marks on it — it really is worth being patient and letting it set at room temperature. But be warned, it can take a while. Patience, they say, is a virtue ... but I'm not so sure!

PEPPERMINT CREAMS

Ingredients

1 large egg white
squeeze of lemon juice
pinch of salt
350g icing sugar, sifted, + extra for dusting
1 tsp peppermint extract

OPTIONAL EXTRAS:

a few drops of green natural food colouring
50g dark chocolate (70% cocoa solids), melted

MAKES 25 -ish

Method

1 Tip the egg white into a large bowl and whisk until it forms soft peaks — which will take a little elbow grease!

2 Next, slowly whisk in a squeeze of lemon juice, the peppermint extract and a pinch of salt.

3 Then use a wooden spoon to gradually incorporate the icing sugar, to make a stiff, thick paste.

4 Here's for the fun part — if you're using green colouring indulge your artistic side now! Split the batch into three portions. Put one third of the mixture aside, to keep it brilliant white. Make the second portion vibrant green by thoroughly beating the colouring in until smooth. Lastly get arty with the final third by very lightly drizzling or dotting in the food colouring — be careful as a little goes a long way — then roll and ripple the mixture to create a marbling effect.

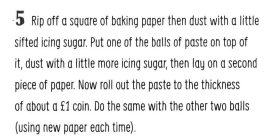

5 Rip off a square of baking paper then dust with a little sifted icing sugar. Put one of the balls of paste on top of it, dust with a little more icing sugar, then lay on a second piece of paper. Now roll out the paste to the thickness of about a £1 coin. Do the same with the other two balls (using new paper each time).

6 Take the paste off the paper and using a 2 or 3cm round cutter, stamp out rounds of the paste and place on a baking tray lined with more baking paper. Re-roll any trimmings and continue until the mixture is used up. Cover with cling film and pop into the fridge to chill for a couple of hours until set.

7 If you want to make some chocolatey, gently melt the chocolate in a heatproof bowl over a saucepan of simmering water. Half-dip some of the peppermint creams in chocolate, or drizzle it over them in artistic patterns. Leave to set again on the baking paper before tucking in.

UPSIDE-DOWN CHERRY LOAF

MAKES 10 slices

Ingredients

FOR THE CAKE:

320g glacé cherries
180g unsalted butter, softened + a bit more for greasing
180g caster sugar
3 large eggs
180g self-raising flour
1 tsp baking powder

few splashes of milk (2–3 tbsp)
1 lemon
50g mixed peel (optional)

FOR THE ICING:

75g icing sugar
splash of water (about 1 tbsp)

You will need a 900g (2lb) loaf tin (23cm x 13cm).

Method

1 Preheat the oven to 180°C (160°C fan/gas mark 4). Grease your loaf tin with butter, then line with baking paper.

2 First, prepare the star ingredient, the cherries! They will be swimming in syrup, so rinse and pat them dry using kitchen paper. Line the base of the tin with the cherries, so they sit in neat rows all the way across the bottom.

3 Beat the butter and sugar together in a large bowl using an electric whisk, until it is soft, light, pale and fluffy. Beat in the eggs one at a time, adding a tablespoon of the flour if the mixture shows any signs of curdling.

4 Fold the remaining flour and baking powder into the mix, adding a few splashes of milk to loosen if necessary.

Finally, fold in the zest (finely grated peel) from the lemon and the mixed peel if using.

5 Spoon into the cherry-lined loaf tin and bake in the preheated oven for approximately 1 hour 10 minutes or until a skewer inserted into the middle comes out clean. Leave to cool for 10 minutes in the tin before turning the loaf out upside down on to a wire rack to cool, so the cherries are sitting on top.

6 To make the drizzle icing, sift the icing sugar into a bowl and trickle in a splash of water (about a tablespoon should do it), stirring as you go until you have a thick paste that just falls nicely off the spoon. Using the back of a spoon, liberally drizzle the icing over the cake with gusto and height, being as creative as you want. Enjoy!

DREAMY HOT CHOCOLATE

MAKES
4 *little mugs*

Ingredients

800ml whole milk

2 strips of orange peel

100g dark chocolate (70% cocoa solids)

100g milk chocolate

4 tbsp double cream + extra for serving (optional)

big handful of mini marshmallows (optional)

Method

1 Pour the milk into a large saucepan set over a medium heat, and drop in the orange peel. Bring the milk to almost boiling, then when it's steaming keep the heat steady and allow the milk to quietly and gently infuse for a few minutes.

2 Roughly chop the dark and milk chocolate into little pieces, saving a little bit to grate on the top at the end.

3 Turn the heat off and use a slotted spoon to lift out the orange peel and chuck it away. Drop the choc chunks in and whisk until it is all melted and silky smooth, then stir in the cream for a little extra richness.

4 Pour the hot chocolate into little mugs. If you're feeling particularly wicked, whip up a little extra cream until peaky, and dollop it on top of your delicious treat ... or chuck a scattering of mini marshmallows on top of each one to get melty-gooey.

5 To finish, finely grate the last of the chocolate over the top.

DREAMY OR WHAT?

HODDER CHILDREN'S BOOKS
First published in Great Britain in 2017 by Hodder & Stoughton
This edition published in 2021

3 5 7 9 10 8 6 4 2

The Famous Five®, The Secret Seven®, Malory Towers®, Magic Faraway Tree®, Enid Blyton®
and Enid Blyton's signature are registered trade marks of Hodder & Stoughton Limited
Recipes and Foreword created and written by Allegra McEvedy
Text © 2017 Hodder & Stoughton Limited
Illustrations © 2017 Hodder & Stoughton Limited

A CIP catalogue record for this book is available from the British Library.

ISBN 978 1 444 93990 3

Designed and art-directed by Lynne Manning
Illustrated by Mark Beech
Photography by Georgia Glynn Smith
Food styling by Lisa Harrison
Edited by Alexandra Antscherl

Printed in China

The paper and board used in this book are made from wood from responsible sources.

MIX
Paper from
responsible sources
FSC® C104740
FSC
www.fsc.org

Hodder Children's Books
An imprint of
Hachette Children's Group
Part of Hodder & Stoughton
Carmelite House
50 Victoria Embankment
London EC4Y 0DZ

An Hachette UK Company
www.hachette.co.uk
www.hachettechildrens.co.uk